....

DEFINE AND RULE

The W. E. B. Du Bois Lectures

....

DEFINE AND RULE

Native as Political Identity

MAHMOOD MAMDANI

Harvard University Press

CAMBRIDGE, MASSACHUSETTS

LONDON, ENGLAND

2012

Library of Congress Cataloging-in-Publication Data

Mamdani, Mahmood, 1946-

Define and rule : native as political

identity / Mahmood Mamdani.—1st ed.

p. cm.

Includes bibliographical references and index.

ISBN 978-0-674-05052-5

1. Colonies—Administration—Philosophy.   2. Colonies—

Administration—History.   3. Decolonization—Philosophy.

4. Decolonization—History.   I. Title.

JV412.M36 2012

325'.3—dc23

2012004821

For Wawa

Contents

DEFINE AND RULE

Introduction

The inspiration for these lectures came from two sources: the first from a reading of W. E. B. Du Bois's *The World and Africa* in 2007.[1] I realized that rather than just write about Africa, Du Bois located Africa in the context of world history. This meant writing about the world from an African vantage point. The second came from a question I was asked by Professor Andreas Eshete, then the vice chancellor at Addis Ababa University, following a lecture I gave on British indirect rule: how, he asked, is this different from previous empires? I gave a long and somewhat convoluted answer, and, maybe just because of that, I left with a distinct feeling that I needed to give serious and further thought to this question.

The focus of these lectures is the indirect rule state, which I have come to understand as a quintessentially modern form of rule in a colonial setting. Indirect rule differed from modes of rule in previous Western empires—including Roman and British "direct" rule before mid-nineteenth century, and French "assimilation" before the early twentieth century turn to "association"—in two important ways. First, previous empires focused on conquered elites rather than the mass of the colonized. Second, they aimed to eradicate difference through a policy of cultural and sometimes political assimilation of colonized elites, whereas indirect rule claimed not just to acknowledge difference but also to shape it.

The management of difference is the holy cow of the modern study of society, just as it is central to modern statecraft. The shift from a homogenizing impulse to a preoccupation with defining and managing difference is most evident in the transition from direct to indirect rule. I argue that it is under indirect rule colonialism that the definition and management of difference was developed as the essence of governance. The difference between the modern democratic state and its colonial version is this: the modern state ensures equal citizenship in political society while acknowledging difference in civil society, but its colonial counterpart institutionalized difference in both the polity and society.

In the colonial indirect rule state, the tendency was to limit citizenship to the settler. I argue that, as a political identity, "native" was the creation of intellectuals of an empire-in-crisis. The key figure was Sir Henry Maine, who reflected on the post-1857 crisis of the British Empire in India. But there were also others, such as Christiaan Snouck Hurgronje, whose object of reflection was the Dutch imperial project in Aceh in the East Indies. Unlike what is commonly thought, native does not designate a condition that is original and authentic. Rather, as in Maine, the native is the creation of the colonial state: colonized, the native is pinned down, localized, thrown out of civilization as an outcast, confined to custom, and then defined as its product.

Under indirect rule, the governance of the native was the prerogative of the *native authority*. As a form of governance, *native administration* claimed to be faithful to tradition and custom, which it defined in the singular, more or less unchanged since time immemorial. No matter its local variations, a core set of rules defined the "customary" in indirect rule colonies. They functioned as the gold standard. The rules concerned land and governance. Land in a colony was defined exclusively as a composite of different homelands, each the home of a designated native tribe. Only those officially designated as natives could claim land rights in the tribal homeland. As a result, participation in public affairs was no longer the right of all those who lived on the land; instead, it became the exclusive preserve of natives said to belong to the homeland. Colonial privilege took two forms: racial and tribal. Both were based on legally sanctioned difference, and both were in turn taken as proof of that difference. If settler cosmopolitanism claimed to be a product of race difference, native particularism was said to reflect the authenticity of the tribe.

Anticolonial nationalism was the antidote to enforced difference; it underlined our common humanity. When it came to the nationalist project, however, there was no agreement. Some sought to turn the world of the settler and the native upside down; others were determined to change it so that both settler and native would cease to exist as political identities. When

3

does a settler become a native?[2] I asked this question in my inaugural lecture at the University of Cape Town in 1998 and answered: never. The only emancipation possible for settler and native is for both to cease to exist as political identities.

Settlers and natives go together: there can be no settler without a native, and vice versa. Either the two are reproduced together, or the two are abolished together. What produces them as political identities is a form of the state that distinguishes settlers from natives in law, at one time valorizing the settler, at another the native. To reform this state and to rewrite the historiography that undergirded the colonial political project and, in the process to historicize "tradition" so as to reclaim it, was the political challenge after independence.

The opening chapter will discuss the mode of indirect rule at its inception, both as an intellectual reflection on the mid-nineteenth-century crisis of empire by one of its seminal thinkers, Sir Henry Maine, and as a set of colonial reforms designed to ameliorate this crisis in India, the British colony of Malaya and the Dutch East Indies. The focus of Chapter 2 is the elaboration of "indirect rule" in the African colonies. I elaborate on one case in particular: colonial Sudan in the aftermath of another major crisis of the empire, the Mahdiyya. The concluding chapters turn to the antithesis of this process: the movement for decolonization, in both its intellectual and political dimensions, first to discuss the equally seminal contribution of a Nigerian historian, Yusuf Bala Usman, who, I argue, provides the intellectual antidote to colonial historiographies,

4

and the statecraft of Mwalimu Julius Nyerere, whose pioneering reforms not only effectively decolonized the indirect rule state but, in so doing, provide us with a nonviolent alternative to a Leninist vision of "smashing" the state. At the same time, these reforms drive a wedge between the nation-building project and the project for democracy and social justice, a question best left for later reflection.

CHAPTER ONE

Nativism: The Theory

Sir Henry Maine and the
Post-1857 Crisis of Empire

A new form of colonial governmentality was born in the aftermath of the mid-nineteenth-century crisis of colonialism. Of the theorists who articulated the response to the crisis, the most important was Sir Henry Maine. Maine sought to recognize the historicity and the agency of the colonized as part of an endeavor to rethink and reconstitute the colonial project on a more durable basis. Through a theory of history and a theory of law, he distinguished the West from the non-West and a universal civilization from local custom. In the process, he distinguished the settler from the native, providing elements of a theory of nativism: if the settler was modern, the native was not; if history defined the settler, geography defined the native; if legislation and sanction defined modern political society, habitual observance defined that of the native. If continuous progress was the mark of settler civilization, native custom was best thought of as part of nature, fixed and unchanging. The native was the creation of theorists of an empire-in-crisis.

Sir Henry Maine became a legal member of the viceroy's cabinet in postmutiny India. His books became compulsory reading for those being groomed for the India Service and,

6

indeed, for the Colonial Service. From Alfred Lyall in India to Frank Swettenham in Malaya, Theophilus Shepstone in Natal, Lord Cromer in Egypt, Frederick Lugard in Nigeria and Uganda, Harold MacMichael in Sudan, and Donald Cameron in Tanganyika, colonial administrators throughout the empire translated the assumptions around which Maine had marshaled his arguments—particularly in his well-known text, *Ancient Law*—into policies. The result was a mode of rule undergirded by a set of institutions—a racialized and tribalized historiography, a bifurcation between civil and customary law, and an accompanying census that classified and enumerated the native population into so many "natural" groups. Transplanted to African colonies in the early twentieth century, the "customary" administrative authority classified the population in each unit ("tribal homeland") into natives and migrants, except this time both were ethnicized rather than racialized, with customary law privileging the ethnic native while discriminating against the ethnic migrant. Excluded from the racialized domain of rights, a theory of history framed the agency of the native, set into motion by the colonial legal system, and targeted by its administrative practice. Cradled by colonial power and scholarship, this agency was said to be tribal. Tribalism is reified ethnicity. It is culture pinned to a homeland, culture in fixity, politicized, so that it does not move.

Its architects claimed this mode of rule was no more than a pragmatic response to a dearth of resources, making for a weak state with a superficial impact, and thus called it "indirect

7

rule." My assessment is the opposite. True, the language of rule was benign: it evolved from a language of "noninterference" in post-1857 India to one of "protection" by the end of the nineteenth century, not only in India, but also in the Malay states and Dutch Indonesia. By the time it was transported to twentieth-century Africa, this mode of rule claimed to preserve custom and tradition through indirect rule. But the indirect rule state was not a weak state. Unlike the preceding era of direct rule, its ambitions were vast: to shape the subjectivities of the colonized population and not simply of their elites.

THE TRANSITION FROM
DIRECT TO INDIRECT RULE

The second half of the nineteenth century witnessed a crisis of empire at both its ends, India and Jamaica, starting with the 1857 uprising in India, known as the Sepoy Mutiny, and closing with Morant Bay in Jamaica in 1865. Together, these developments made for a crisis of mission and a crisis of justification. In the reflection that followed the crisis, the colonial mission was redefined—from civilization to conservation and from progress to order.

Between 1757 and 1857, two-thirds of the landmass of South Asia had been brought under Company rule, either directly as subjects or, indirectly, as princes under protective custody. The main outlines of the Utilitarian and evangelical agenda were clear by 1850: to abolish the Moghul court and to

8

impose British laws and technology—along with Christianity—on India. Then in 1857, all but 7,796 of the 139,000 *sepoys* of the Bengal Army turned against their British masters.[1] The civilizing mission, spearheaded by liberal Utilitarians and Christian evangelists, had faltered. Why? It was, in Maine's words, the result of a failure of analysis; a failure to understand the nature of "native Indian religious and social belief." Maine argued that this "vast" subject had been "so superficially examined" that "I insist on the necessity of having some accurate ideas about it, and on the fact that a mistake about [it] caused the Sepoy Mutiny."[2]

What was this "defect of knowledge?" It was twofold. The first was an over-reliance on Sanskrit texts while underplaying the importance of everyday practice: "nothing can give a falser impression of the actual Brahminical religion than the sacred Brahminical literature. It represents itself as an organized religious system, whereas its true peculiarity, and (I may add) its chief interest, arises from its having no organization whatever."[3] Maine called for a shift of focus, away from the Orientalist preoccupation with texts, to observing daily life. The logic of native institutions, Maine argued, was to be found in local customs and traditions. The problem was that even when Orientalists tried to understand daily life, they made the mistake of focusing on the more urbanized and cosmopolitan coast as opposed to the more rural and traditional hinterland, simply because the former was more accessible and the latter more isolated. He cited as examples the highly influential *Histoire*

Philosophique des deux Indes by Abbe Raynal and Diderot, the eighteenth-century French philosophical account of India, as well as less influential English writings, such as Mr. Buckle's *History of Civilisation*. They had failed to understand "the extreme isolation of the country until it was opened up by maritime adventure," the reason why "all things Aryan, the chief part of the heritage of the greatest of races, are older in India than elsewhere."[4]

For India's historic isolation, Maine gave two reasons. The first was geography: "Approached not by sea but by land, there is no portion of the earth into which it is harder to penetrate." The second "powerful preservative has been the influence of Religion and Caste." Whereas geographical isolation accounted for the paucity of external influence, Maine argued that caste and religion accounted for the lack of change internally: "Brahminism is in fact essentially a religion of compromise. . . . Thus Brahminism does not destroy but preserves old beliefs and cults, and with them the institutions which many of them consecrate and hold together. It cannot be doubted that Central India thus reproduces the old heathen world which Christianity destroyed. . . . Thus, ancient practices and customs, little protected by law, have always been protected by religion."[5] Indeed, argued Maine, "the primitive Aryan groups, the primitive Aryan institutions, the primitive Aryan ideas have really been arrested in India at an early stage of development," so much so that, "a large part of ancient Europe survives in India."[6]

Maine went on to paint the contrast between the coast and the hinterland in the sharpest possible colors, portraying the two as disconnected realities. He argued strenuously that it was wrong to generalize from the coast to India as a whole: "For it is in the cities of the coast and their neighborhood that there has sprung up, under English influence, a thirst for knowledge, a body of opinions, and a standard of taste, which are wholly new in India. There you may see universities thronged like the European schools of the later middle age. There you may observe an eagerness in the study of Western literature and science not very unlike the enthusiasm of European scholars at the revival of letters. From this part of India come those most interesting samples of the native race who from time to time visit this country; but they are a growth of the coast, and there could be no greater mistake than to generalize from them as to the millions upon millions of men who fill the vast interior of India."[7]

Maine urged the reader to pass "beyond the fringe of British civilization which is found at certain points of the Indian coast" and "enter this great interior block," declaring: "No doubt the social state there to be observed can only be called Barbarism, if we only get rid of unfavorable associations with the word." Ignored by the European literati, this India "has been most carefully observed and described by English functionaries from the administrative point of view ... in hundreds of reports." And so concluded Maine: "There is no doubt that this is the real India, its barbarism (if I must use the word) imperceptibly giving way in the British territories until it ends at the coast in a dissolution amid which something like a likeness of our own civilization may be discerned."[8] Woe be it to the Utilitarians who, in ignorance of this "real India," had concluded "that Indians require nothing but School Boards and Normal Schools to turn them into Englishmen."[9]

Maine cast the contrast between the cosmopolitan coast and the isolated hinterland as one between an impure coast, open to foreign influences, and the pure hinterland whose isolation had protected it from contamination by these same influences. The same observer who would habitually recount the history of the English coast, open to foreign influences from the time of the Romans, as a story of progress, took a dim view of outside influences buffeting the Indian coast.

Maine did more than just lay the conceptual foundation and intellectual justification of indirect rule. He laid claim to founding a new comparative science, one that he referred to as comparative jurisprudence. This is how he put it in his 1875 Rede lecture before the University of Cambridge: "India has given to the world Comparative Philology and Comparative Mythology; it may yet give us a new science not less valuable than the sciences of language and of folk-lore. I hesitate to call it Comparative jurisprudence because, if it ever exists, its area will be so much wider than the field of law."[10]

Maine argued for a more intimate and local understanding of native society, in particular, of institutions that he identified as religion and caste. In doing so, he contrasted "real India"

with the India of "Brahminical theory" embraced by Orientalists. Claiming that natives were attached to local custom, not
universal ideas or ideals, Maine argued for understanding caste
as lived at the local level, as *jati*, and not in universal terms as
varna, as did the Orientalists. He told his Oxford audience: "I
am aware that the popular impression here is that Indian
society is divided, so to speak, into a number of horizontal
strata, each representing a caste. This is an entire mistake. It is
extremely doubtful whether the Brahminical theory of caste
upon caste was ever true except of the two highest castes; and
it is even likely that more importance has been attached to it in
modern than ever was in ancient times. The real India con-
tains one priestly caste, which in a certain, though a very limited, sense is the highest of all, and there are, besides, some
princely houses and a certain number of tribes, village communities and guilds, which still in our day advance a claim,
considered by many good authorities extremely doubtful, to
belong to the second or the third of the castes recognized by
the Brahminical writers. But otherwise, caste is merely a name
for trade or occupation, and the sole tangible effect of the
Brahminical theory is that it creates a religious sanction for
what is really a primitive and natural distribution of classes."[11]

The more he theorized the local, the more Maine went on
to closet the native in a separate conceptual world, shut off
from the world of the settler by a binary: progressive and stationary societies. Maine was of course not the only one to
think of the modern as a sharp break from the traditional. The

nineteenth century saw the explosion of historical and anthropological research on the non-European world, leading to the development of social theory (classical sociology) and evolutionary anthropology.[12] From this intellectual ferment was born the social theory of Ferdinand de Tonnies, turning on a contrast between *Gemeinschaft* and *Gesellschaft*, and that of Emile Durkheim, its focus on the difference between mechanical and organical solidarity. Maine, however, highlighted a different binary, one that distinguished the West from the non-West, which he sometimes called the East.

If the social became the privileged theoretical arena for understanding the nature and dynamics of society in the West, that privilege was given to the domain of culture in the non-West. Thus was born a bifurcated notion of culture, said to be a walled, isolated, and unchanging affair in the non-West, as opposed to a transformative one in the West.[13] The native was said to represent a triumph of geography over time. India, from this point of view, resembled a house of custom, so complacent that geography could be said to signify history: "There is no country, probably, in which custom is so stable as it is in India."[14]

Maine underpinned this binary with a theory of legal evolution. He claimed that law in its first stage had evolved from an unwritten customary affair to written codes[15] and that this had been the work of aristocracies. The difference was that "in the East aristocracies became religious, in the West civil or political."[16] This is why the code in the West was an account of rules actually observed, but that in the East was idealized: the idealization being religious in India and nonreligious in China.[17] The difference arose from one in circumstance: whereas the Roman Code was compiled *before* corruption set in, the codes in the East were compiled *after* corruption had set in.[18] Maine contended that "the question . . . which affected the whole future of each community . . . was not so much whether there should be a code at all, for the majority of ancient societies seemed to have obtained them sooner or later." He went on to elaborate the real issue: "But the point on which turned the history of the race was, at what period, at what stage of their social progress, they should have their laws put into writing."

It seems the difference in timing arose from a political difference: "In the Western world the plebeian or popular element in each State successfully assailed the oligarchical monopoly, and a code was nearly universally obtained *early* in the history of the Commonwealth. But, in the East . . . the ruling oligarchies tended to become religious rather than military or political, and gained, therefore, rather than lost in power."[19] This difference in timing had a telling effect: "The rigidity of primitive law, arising chiefly from its early association and identification with religion, has chained down the mass of the human race to those views of life and conduct which they entertained at the time when their usages were first consolidated into a systematic form."[20] There was also a secondary difference between India and China. Whereas the association and identification with religion was primarily responsible for the rigidity of primitive law in India, that same rigidity arose in China from a more secular tendency to idealize law.[21]

Maine's larger point was that the West represented an exception in human social evolution. From the standpoint of world history, only the West could claim to be the site for the development of progress: ". . . the stationary condition of the human race is the rule, the progressive the exception."[22] Maine set out to understand the historical factors that explain the difference between the "progressive" West and the "stationary" non-West: "In spite of overwhelming evidence, it is most difficult for a citizen of Western Europe to bring thoroughly home to himself the truth that the civilization which surrounds him is a rare exception in the history of the world." To reflect on this rare achievement is, indeed, to think through "the relation of the progressive races to the totality of human life."[23] The difference between the two was not just legal; it was, rather, a difference in moral and political order. The place of kinship in stationary societies signified that difference.

Kinship was for Maine the central political fact of primitive society. "It is often said," wrote Maine in *Lectures on the Early History of Institutions* (1875), "that it takes two or three years before a Governor General learns that the vast Indian population is an aggregate of natural groups and not the mixed multitude he left at home; and some rulers of India have been accused of never having mastered the lesson at all."[24] This "natural group" was kinship: "The most recent researches into the primitive history of society point to the conclusion that the earliest tie which knitted men together in communities was Consanguinity or Kinship."[25] But, kinship, Maine recognized, functioned not literally but as the prototype of what he would later characterize as legal fiction, a highly elastic notion that could be stretched to fit changing circumstances. It designated as kinfolk not only those who were indeed blood relations but also those enslaved, abducted, and incorporated into the original group for a variety of reasons. Kinship thus designated "groups of men either in fact united by blood-relationship, or believing or assuming that they are so united."[26]

Maine saw kinship as the foundation of the original political community. "The history of political ideas begins with the assumption that kinship in blood is the sole possible ground of community in political functions."[27] Kin relations are at the same time relations of power: "Kinship, as the tie binding communities together, tends to be regarded as the same thing with subjection to a common authority. The notions of Power and Consanguinity blend, but they in no wise supersede one another."[28] This is why ancient society was not a collection of individuals but an aggregation of families, "with one peculiarity invariably distinguishing the infancy of society. Men are regarded and treated, not as individuals, but always as members of a particular group."[29] In fact, he emphasized, "ancient law . . . knows next to nothing of Individuals."[30]

Maine argued that without the double function of kinship—both designating a principle and providing a flexible practical device for absorption of new groups—it would be difficult to see how primitive groups could have expanded in scale. He called this double function by the name *Legal Fiction:* "If it had never existed, I do not see how any one of the primitive groups, whatever were their nature, could have absorbed another, or on what terms any two of them could have combined, except those of absolute superiority on one side and absolute subjection on the other."[31] Indeed, "the expedient which in those times commanded favor was that the incoming population should feign themselves to be descended from the same stock as the people on whom they were engrafted; and it is precisely the good faith of this fiction, and the closeness with which it seemed to imitate reality, that we cannot now hope to understand."[32]

In *Lectures on the Early History of Institutions,* Maine provided the building blocks of social evolution, tracing the line of development from tribe to race: "The tribes of men with which the student of jurisprudence is concerned are exclusively those belonging to the races now universally classed, on the ground of linguistic affinities, as Aryan and Semitic."[33] As he focused on the history of the Aryan race, Maine asked why certain of its branches (Ireland and India in particular) have not participated in the story of progress that has been the driving force of the history of the West. Between the Irish and the Indian experiences, he found numerous similarities.[34] But the most important, and determining, was the fact that neither was subject to—and thus benefited from—"the influence, direct and indirect, of the Roman Empire."[35] Maine was convinced that the present of the more backward societies is a sure clue to the past of the more progressive ones "when we are occupied with the investigation of the laws of progress": "the primitive condition of the progressive societies is best ascertained from the observable condition of those which are nonprogressive."[36] And so he looked to contemporary Ireland and India for clues to the more obscure aspects of English history.

If Ireland and India represented cases of arrested development, a tendency to which England was the exception, then the reason for it must be the tendency to idealize law in both Ireland and India. While Maine conceded that the ancient Brehon law in Ireland "possessed great authority," he argued that "it was in all probability irregularly and intermittently enforced, and that partial and local departures from it were common all over ancient Ireland." Similarly, "with the infinity of local usage practiced in India," it would not be a surprise for a student of India to be "constantly asking himself how far was the law of the Brahmin jurists observed before the English undertook to enforce it through their tribunals."[37] Herein lay the answer for why both ancient Ireland and pre-British India had yet to move from customary to civil law.

From Customary to Civil Law

Maine argued, "the movement of the progressive societies has hitherto been a movement *from Status to Contract*."[38] It is the difference between two kinds of laws—one custom-bound, the other abstract—that explained the divide between progressive and stationary societies. This is how the central argument went: as a rule, and so with humanity at large, the development of law was culture-bound ("customary" law), but a small minority of Europeans had succeeded in developing an abstract law ("civil" law), one that was free of time and circumstance and so could truly be the basis of a universal civilizing mission. Whereas customary law was context-bound, civil law had transcended context. Whereas customary law was as rooted in the ground as the peasant and his crops, civil law could travel globally. The problem in India, as elsewhere outside the West, was that "instead of the civilization expanding the law, the law has limited the civilization."[39]

The division between customary and modern law drove Maine's theorization. Customary law holds civilization back; because of its attachment to culture, law chains society to a particular point in time. "Progressive" law stands for that law that responds to advances in civilization; by removing the connection between law and culture, law is liberated. Abstracting law makes it an instrument of progress. Thus we have the duality between two kinds of laws: culture-free in the West, and culture-bound outside it[40] and, based on this legal duality, two kinds of societies: progressive and stationary.

It is from this theoretical platform that Maine launched his main critique of the civilizing mission associated with the Utilitarians "who thought that political institutions could be imported like steam machinery, warranted to stand any climate and benefit every community."[41]

Tribal and Modern Sovereignty

Maine's political critique of Utilitarians counterposed a historical account of sovereignty to what he claimed were John Austin's philosophical abstractions. The problem with the "Austinian view of Sovereignty," argued Maine, is that "it is the result of Abstraction," a process that focuses on the result by dismissing "the entire history of each community."[42] The "practical value" of such a method "depends on the relative importance of the elements rejected and the elements retained in the process of abstraction."[43] This, indeed, was why "the pupil of Austin may be tempted to forget that there is more in actual Sovereignty than force, and more in laws which are the commands of Sovereigns than . . . regulated force."[44] Precisely because Austin focused on jurisprudence—"the science of Positive Law . . . Commands, addressed by Sovereigns to their Subjects, imposing a Duty, or condition of obligedness, or obligation, on those Subjects, and threatening a Sanction, or Penalty, in the event of disobedience to the Command"[45]—he risked forgetting "that great mass of rules, which men in fact obey, which have some of the characteristics of laws, but which are not (as such) imposed by Sovereigns on subjects, and which are not (as such) enforced by the sanction supplied by Sovereign power."[46] Even if "sovereignty is from the nature of the case incapable of legal limitation," there are other nonlegal, historical limitations on sovereignty: "sovereigns are restrained from issuing some commands and determined to issue others by rules which, though they are not laws, are of extreme cogency."[47]

Maine illustrated his point, thus: "The Tyrant of a Greek city often satisfied every one of Austin's tests of Sovereignty; yet it was part of the accepted definition of a Tyrant that he subverted the laws."[48] To drive it home, he gave an Indian example, that of Raja Ranjeet Singh of the Sikhs, "absolutely despotic . . . he kept the most perfect order. . . . Yet I doubt whether once in all his life he issued a command which Austin would call a law."[49] Though "he never made a law . . . the rules which regulated the life of his subjects were derived from their immemorial usages, and these rules were administered by domestic tribunals, in families or village-communities."[50] The significance of the example, said Maine, is that "the Punjaub under Runjeet Singh may be taken as a type of all Oriental communities in their native state, during their rare intervals of peace and order."[51] The example of Raja Ranjeet Singh, for Maine, captured the essence of a premodern political society: "It is important to observe that, for the purposes of the present inquiry, the state of political society which I have described as Indian or Oriental is a far more trustworthy clue to the former condition of the greatest part of the world than is the modern social organization of Western Europe, as we see it before our eyes."[52]

As with law, so with political society, Maine drove a wedge between two types: modern and premodern: "There are thus two types of organized political society. In the more ancient of these, the great bulk of men derive their rules of life from the customs of their village or city, but they occasionally, though most implicitly, obey the commands of an absolute ruler who takes taxes from them but never legislates. In the other, and the one with which we are most familiar, the Sovereign is ever more actively legislating on principles of his own, while local custom and idea are ever hastening to decay."[53] Austin had focused on the modern polity and civil law, but he had little insight to offer on how to govern a premodern polity organized along customary lines. "Customary law—a subject in which all of Austin's remarks seem to me comparatively unfruitful—is not obeyed, as enacted law is obeyed."[54] In other words, custom is *observed*, laws are *obeyed*.

Absorbed in their philosophical abstractions, the Utilitarians had mistaken the world—in particular the colonies—for the West writ large. More than any other event, 1857 had exposed the grave consequences of this folly: "As has been truly said, the British rulers of India are like men bound to make their watches keep true time in two longitudes at once. Nevertheless the paradoxical position must be accepted. If they are too slow, there will be no improvement. If they are too fast, there will be no security. The true solution of the problem will be found, I believe, in some such examination and classification of Indian phenomena as that of which I have been venturing to affirm the possibility. Those who, guided solely by Western social experience, are too eager for innovations which seem to them indistinguishable from improvements, will perhaps be overtaken by a wholesale distrust when they see in institutions and customs, which would otherwise appear to them ripe for destruction, the materials of knowledge by which the Past, and to some extent the Present, of the West may be interpreted. On the other hand, though it be virtually impossible to reconcile the great majority of the natives of India to the triumph of Western ideas, maxims, and practices, which is nevertheless inevitable, we may at all events say to the best and the most intelligent of them that we do not innovate or destroy in mere arrogance. We rather change because we cannot help it."[55]

Maine's debate with the Utilitarians was not about the fact of change but about its pace. His object was not to prevent change, as the notion of conserving custom may suggest to some; rather, he called for a determined slowing down of change in the colonial context. Here, from Maine's point of view, lay the crux of the problem. When authority emanates from a source external to the small natural group, when laws that command replace rules that call forth observance, without the support of habit, opinion, and spontaneity, law and sovereignty appear both external and coercive.[56] In traditional society, the dull "despotism of usage" (custom) outside the family contrasted with the active "despotism of paternal authority" within the *patria potestas*. The transfer of active authority from the family to the sovereign power was the result of radically changed conditions: "Their generality and their dependence on the coercive force of a Sovereign are the result of the great territorial area of modern States, of the comminution of the sub-groups which compose them, and above all of the example and influence of the Roman Commonwealth under Assembly, Senate, and Prince, which from the very early times was distinguished from all other dominations and powers in that it brake up more thoroughly that which it devoured."[57] Distinctive to modern politics is a legislature. Not surprisingly, the theory of utility—the greatest happiness of the greatest number—presupposes both a theory of equality and the universalism of modern legislation. Maine stopped there. But he could as well have continued: active sovereignty requires democracy to produce order, which is why colonial order requires that colonial power not only harness the dull compulsion of custom but claim it as justification for power.

Maine agreed with the Utilitarians that rulers in traditional India did not legislate. They issued commands but not laws. In that sense, they were not sovereign. For sovereignty is a territory that circulates laws issued by a sovereign. The new science of jurisprudence, of which Maine claimed to be the originator, held that natives may have their own history, but they do not have access to their history. Such access requires science, key to which is the ability to theorize. Thus Maine held the epistemological agency—the key—to unlocking the secret of native history. Europeans needed to recognize that India has always been ruled by custom, never by a sovereign. This was why rule through legislation was bound to turn into a daily and unpleasant reminder to Indians that they lived under foreign, Western rule. It was also why in India good governance was local governance, decentralized governance, and customary governance.

RESPONSE TO MUTINY

The gist of British response to the Mutiny came in the form of a doctrine contained in Queen Victoria's Proclamation of 1858. This was the doctrine of noninterference in the private domain, especially in religion:[58]

> [w]e declare it our royal will and pleasure that none be in anywise favoured, none molested or disquieted, by reason of their religious faith or observances, but that all shall alike enjoy the equal and impartial protection of the law; and we do strictly charge to enjoin all those who may be in authority under us that they abstain from all interference with the religious belief or worship of any of our subjects on pain of our highest displeasure.

The doctrine of noninterference turned into a charter for all around interference for one reason: the occupying power gave itself the prerogative to define the boundaries of that in which it will *not* interfere, and then to define the content of the authentic religion with which there was to be *no* interference, and finally, to acknowledge the authentic authority that would define and safeguard religion in its pure form—without external interference. The prerogative to define the boundary, the substance and the authority of the "customary," gave vast scope to the powers of the occupying authority. But the exercise of this power, the list of those to be "protected," was politically determined—and it grew as time passed.

The first round was about setting limits on the operation of the market, thereby protecting the village community from moneylenders, agricultural subcastes from trading castes, and the landlord's estate from division and fragmentation.[59] Maine's "functionalism-before-the-term-was-invented" rehabilitated the village community, the subcaste, and the feudal estate by showing that each and every mechanism had definite functions to fulfill. Invested with a "manifest social purpose," each stopped being a social anachronism.[60] In the second round, protection was extended to groups in civil society, first to Muslims in the 1880s and 1890s, then to Sikhs, then to non-Brahmin groups, then to Hill Peoples.[61] Over time, this list looked like an imperial charter to protect minorities from majorities. Rather than the mission of colonial rule, its agenda, the protection of minorities, turned into its rationale.

It is instructive to recall the debate in British Indian circles on how to respond to Muslim organization and representation in Bengal in the late-nineteenth century. Faced with growing agitation, there was agreement within British ranks that there was no choice but to extend representation to Muslims. The debate was on the terms of that representation: should it be

territorial or group-based? When it came to the Partition of
Bengal in 1905, the choice was not only stark but also of great
historical significance. John Morley, Secretary of State for India,
proposed territorial representation in light of agitation over the
1905 partition and the Swadeshi movement of 1905 to 1908. He
was opposed by the director of ethnography, Risley, now Home
Secretary to the Indian government, who proposed group representation based on the demand of the newly formed Muslim
League for separate electorates. Awarded in the Morley-Minto
reforms of 1909, group representation fueled the demand for a
renewed partition, this time beyond Bengal.[62]

THE REGIME OF PROTECTION
BECAME A TECHNOLOGY OF GOVERNANCE

Conservation and protection of institutions and groups was in
reality a strategy to contain social and political change. Brought
under critical scrutiny, the civilizing mission of the pre-1857
era—in reality a set of changes from the market to rule of law
to an evangelizing Christianity—had unleashed a destructive
influence on "custom" and "tradition." Threatened by unchecked
modernity, tradition, custom, and its bearer, the native, was
said to be in dire need of protection. Hence, the colonial mission shifted from civilization to preservation and from assimilation to protection.

A two-pronged initiative set this shift in motion: legal and
administrative, unfolding simultaneously in the decade between

1862 and 1872. The legal reforms made for a sharp distinction between the public and the private. All traces of Islamic law were removed from the public sphere through a series of legislative changes, ranging from the Indian Penal Code and the Code of Criminal Procedure (1862), which "removed the last traces of Islamic law in the criminal field" to the removal of all Persian titles and the disbarring of all Muslim assistants to the colonial courts (1864) as prelude to the creation of a single legal bureaucracy. At the same time, the reforms of 1862 promulgated multiple personal codes: "one code for each recognized religious group." Aptly summed up by Scott Alan Kugle, "This sealed the division between Hindu and Muslim, and in addition broke the Muslim community into its constituent 'sects,' each with its own code of law."[63] The period after 1857 marked a sharp break in the legal sphere between the Moghul polity and British rule. When it came to non-Muslim communities, Moghul policy left each community "to administer its own law to its own members through its own specialists as long as the community maintained certain limits on public religious practices and offered up financial compensation in taxes." The big difference with British rule was that "the Mughal polity never took up as a state project to administer a community's laws to that community."[64] Whereas the Moghuls, like the Ottomans, related to communities as historically defined, the British actively defined and shaped community identities.

In the period that followed, the native was classified and reclassified, each time in response to political necessity, but always in the language of cultural difference and cosmopolitan tolerance. Claiming to protect authenticity against the threat of progress, the settler defined and pinned the native.

It is in this context that we can see the census as a political device or, more accurately, a technical complement to a political agenda. It named the objects of state policy—both those to be targeted and those to be protected. The "martial races"— in Nick Dirks's words, "Macaulay's hyperbolic denunciation of effeminate Bengalis"[65]—were classified in 1857. The 1872 decennial survey classified Indian society first and foremost according to a single identity: caste, while locating it within a larger setting, village, race, *and* religion. The regime of protection was inaugurated with the Indian Councils Act of 1909, also known as the Morley-Minto Reforms. For the first time, separate electorates were created in the provincial and central legislative bodies: not only were reserved seats created for Muslims in the councils, this reservation also went alongside another: only Muslims were entitled to vote in the competition over these seats. The presumption "that only a Muslim could represent Muslims, or protect Muslim interests . . . would shape political life in India for decades to come."[66] Over time, caste identification became the basis of quotas and reservations for non-Brahmin and scheduled castes, for tribes and for Muslims, in the domains of electoral representation, government jobs, and entry to educational institutions. Nick Dirks has rightly argued that anthropology supplanted history as the principal colonial modality of knowledge and rule after 1857, creating an ethnographic state in late-nineteenth- and early-twentieth-century India.[67] Having characterized colonized societies as stationary, all efforts were invested in containing social change in these societies—and justifying it as *protection* of vulnerable minorities.

By the end of the century, as Maine's texts became required reading for the Indian Civil Service, his influence trickled down to all levels of the service. That influence was most highlighted in the work of administrators such as Alfred Lyall in India, Frank Swettenham in the Malay states, Lord Cromer, Lord Lugard, Theophilus Shepstone, and Harold MacMichael in the African colonies. I shall further illustrate the point with the example of the Malay states.

MALAYA: DISTINGUISHING
CIVILIZED FROM ABORIGINAL NATIVES

Swettenham put the regime of protection into effect in Malaya. It turned around a definition of two different kinds of natives: aboriginal and civilized. The 1874 Treaty of Pangkor, which marked the beginning of British colonization of the Malay states, officially defined a Malay as "one who habitually speaks Malay, professes the religion of Islam and practices Malay customs." This definition continues to be enshrined in Article 160 of the Malay Constitution.[68] The official declaration had a double effect. One, it allowed for many immigrant Muslims to be assimilated into the Malay identity. As a result, Muslim migrants from near and far—from the surrounding Dutch East Indies archipelago to the Arab peninsula—were able to *masuk Melayu* ("become Malay") through the adoption of the Malay language *(bahasa)* and custom *(adat)*.[69] Two—and this was its opposite effect—it turned non-Muslims who had hitherto been as Malay as Muslim Malays into the aborigines they are considered to be today.[70] Why the necessity to define Malay when there had been no such need before? The answer lay in the domain of the political.

The definition of non-Muslim tribes as "aboriginal" did not happen until the Emergency. Prior to the Emergency, there had been a racist naming game in which anthropologists and administrators employed a wide variety of terms to refer to different tribes. Some were named after where they lived, as in Orang Hulu (people of the headwaters), Orang Darat (people of the hinterland), and Orang Laut (people of the sea). Yet others were named to highlight presumably biological characteristics, as in Orang Besisi (people with scales) and Orang Mantra (people who chanted). And yet others were given outright derogatory names, as in Orang Mawas (people like apes), Orang Liar (uncivilized, but free men), and Orang Jinak (tame or enslaved men).[71]

The need to give these tribes a single name arose in the context of an anti-colonial insurgency that coincided with an inter-imperialist war. British strategy was to separate rebels from villagers and forest peoples. Following the Japanese invasion of Malaya in 1941, many of the tribal groups retreated into the jungle where they shared the forests with the Malayan People's Army, a communist-dominated guerrilla force that formed the only effective resistance to the Japanese. As part of the counterinsurgency operation against the communists obtaining assistance from villagers and jungle-dwelling peoples, the British declared the tribes "aboriginal" and appointed them an advisor. The tribes were resettled, at the same time as over 600,000 Chinese squatters were relocated into "new villages." The Department of Orang Asli (meaning, original native, aboriginal) Affairs (JHEOA) was established in 1950, and the Aboriginal People's Ordinance, the first and main piece of legislation concerned with Orang Asli was enacted in 1954. The process continued after independence, with the creation of three distinct political identities: Malay, aboriginal, and *bhumiputera* ("sons of the soil").

The political order established at independence in 1957 distinguished between two groups of Malay: the Muslim ("Malay") and the non-Muslim ("Orang Asli"). The two categories were identified with different rungs of the racial ladder: whereas Muslim Malay were officially acknowledged as civilized, civilized by religion; the Orang Asli, the aboriginal native, was consigned to the lowest rung of the civilizational ladder. The civilized natives were not shy about claiming an exogenous origin, for it only served to confirm their right to rule, whereas the fully indigenous *(asli)* status of the Orang Asli implied that they are only fit to be subjects.[72] That order was reorganized following the race riots of 1969, widely understood to be an

33

expression of Malay marginality in the national socioeconomic order. The New Economic Policy of 1971 conferred special privileges on those regarded *bhumiputera* ("sons of the soil"), a term that covered a variety of groups: Malays, Orang Asli, and various *pribumi* (native) groups. There followed a constitutional amendment that criminalized public discussion of "sensitive" issues; that is, issues relating to the privileged position of Malays in law, the role of Malay sultans, the status of Malay as the official language and Islam as the official religion—and the questioning of Malay privileges.[73]

INDONESIA: DISTINGUISHING
ADAT FROM RELIGIOUS LAW

A few decades after Sir Henry Maine, but with ideas not very different from his, came a Dutch Arabicist and Islamologist, Christiaan Snouck Hurgronje (1857–1936). Like Maine, Hurgronje's contribution, too, came in the aftermath of a crisis, when imperial power turned to this scholar for expert advice on how to deal with the uprising that had begun in Aceh in northern Sumatra in the third quarter of the nineteenth century and lasted for a full three decades under the banner of an Islamic insurgency.[74] It is against this background that Snouck Hurgronje was appointed in 1891 to the newly created office of Advisor on Native and Islamic Affairs. The political reorientation he engineered led to dramatic policy changes, including the codification of custom *(adat)* as law. Even though these changes happened after his departure from the scene and at the initiative of another colonial official, Van Vollenhoven, Hurgronje is credited with the analytical insights behind the policy changes that brought the Aceh War to a successful conclusion.

When Snouck Hurgronje arrived in Aceh in 1891 to "make a special study of the religious element in the political conditions of that country," the Dutch were in their eighteenth year of what seemed to be a war without end.[75] Snouck's main contribution was twofold: to disentangle Islam from a secular history he named "tradition," and to identify separate custodians of each as two separate hierarchies, which later colonial officials eventually played off against each other. It was, in essence, a counterinsurgency project based on identifying and separating friends from enemies.

Hurgronje developed the dichotomy between customary law *(adat)* and religious Islamic law *(hukom)* in his classic work, *The Achehnese*. Hurgronje adapted the notion of *adat* from the Arabic word "*ada*, which refers to ordinary practices or habits which are not addressed in Islamic law." He used *adat* to refer to "custom" or "tradition."[76] *Adat* is worldly; *hukom* is not. Hukom is written and thus easy to identify, *adat* is not and thus difficult to discern: "As a general rule we do not sufficiently reflect that in countries of the standard of civilization reached by the Malayan races, the most important laws are those which are not set down in writing but find their expression, sometimes in proverbs and familiar sayings, but always and above all in the actual occurrences of daily life which appeal to the comprehension of all. . . . We arrive at them only after painstaking and scientific research."[77] *Adat* changes, *hukom* is dogmatic. "In contrast to the changeableness of the individual, the *adat* presents itself as something abiding and incontrovertible, with which the individual may not meddle; yet the *adat* changes like all other worldly things with every successive generation—nay, it never remains stationary for a moment. Even natives, whose intelligence is above the ordinary, know this well and use it to further their own purposes."[78] A few pages later, Hurgronje reiterated the point in unqualified terms: "It must be born in mind that even the most primitive societies and the laws that govern them never remain stationary."[79] If *adat* reflected on-the-ground responsiveness, Hurgronje painted the religious law of Islam as unworldly and unchanging: ". . . the Mohammedan law is unfitted for the practical administration of justice. Among other reasons because it greatly hampers the detection of crime, imposes impossible demands on witnesses and fails to take cognizance of historical changes."[80]

The problem in Aceh and in the East Indies, as Hurgronje saw it, was that the two legacies—one customary *(adat)* and the other religious *(hukom)*, the former flexible and the latter dogmatic—had become intertwined over time: "so far we have learnt of the indissoluble union and indispensable cooperation of *hukom* or religious law with *adat*, the custom of the country, as being the very basis of life in Acheh." Hurgronje suggested a particular way of thinking about the tension produced by this "indissoluble union and indispensable cooperation": "At the same time we have constantly remarked how the *adat* assumes the part of the mistress and the *hukom* that of her obedient slave. The *hukom* however revenges herself over her subordination whenever she sees the chance; her representatives are always on the look-out for an opportunity to escape from this servile position."[81]

Hurgronje looked for a way of undoing the otherwise "indissoluble union" between *adat* and *hukom*. He suggested a twofold strategy. On the one hand, he called for a reform of *adat*, but not that of *hukom*. This differentiated strategy would be the result of a differentiated policy: he called on the Dutch to distinguish between the Islamic scholars *(ulama)* and the customary chiefs *(uleebalang)* and advocated that Dutch power support *adat* chiefs *(uleebalang)* against the Islamic *ulama*. "The uleebalangs . . . are the lords of the country; they are the territorial chiefs par excellence."[82] Hurgronje warned that any attempt to reform religious law would lead to political disaster for it would undermine the *uleebalang* chiefs: "A reformation of the institutions of the country conducted in a religious spirit would rob the uleebalangs of everything. Even if the work were carried out in conformity with the national character of the Achehnese, still the whole administration of justice now in the hands of these chiefs, and which forms the main source of their revenues, would pass entirely away from their control. . . . It is thus not to be wondered that the chiefs view the advancement of the 'upholders of religion' with inward vexation and alarm."[83] The way forward lay in recognizing that *hukom* was not negotiable, whereas *adat* was: "All that belongs to the first of these two categories must be accepted unconditionally by every good Mohameddan."[84] Hurgronje's political project was two-fold: to reform *adat* and, at the same time, reify *hukom*.

Adat could be engaged and reformed, but *hukom* would have to be confronted and subordinated to modern power: "Circumstances have imposed on the Dutch nation the task of impressing this modern doctrine on the Achehnese."[85] Hurgronje assured the Dutch that they had both friends and enemies among the Achehnese; their challenge was to ally themselves with potential friends, in this case the *uleebalang* and the masses (whose interests are "identical" with the invading power), while isolating the small group of "unappeasable fanatics spurred by the ulamas."[86] He insisted that no matter how intertwined Islam and *adat* may be in practice, the Dutch had no choice but to unravel the unity and present each in its purity. In so doing, he ended up creating the opposition that he claimed to exist from time immemorial.

On the other hand—and this was the second part of his twofold strategy—Hurgronje called on the Dutch to distinguish between Islam as a religion and Islam as a political ideology, warning the Dutch authorities that the latter could only be isolated if ordinary Muslims were first assured religious tolerance. The enemy, argued Hurgronje, was not Islam as a religion but Islam as a political doctrine: "The circumstances attending the origin and early development of Islam have rendered it par excellence a militant religion, whose aim was no less than to convert all who held other beliefs or else reduce them to subjection. The teaching of law, as it moulded itself by degrees, comprises a two-fold obligation to activity in the holy war." The first is "the joint and several obligation of the community at large to spread among all others by force of arms, at the bidding of their Chief, the religion or at any rate the sovereignty of the Moslims." The second is "the personal obligation resting on all fighting men, nay in some cases even on the non-combatant inhabitants of a Mohameddan country to defend their land to the utmost against the *invasion* of a non-Mohameddan enemy."[87]

Based on this dualistic understanding of Islam, Hurgronje counseled toleration of the religion but ruthless suppression of any ideologically driven Islamic political movement. He argued that a policy of neutrality toward religious life was the prerequisite for successful pacification and stability. The determined application of the twin policies of tolerance and vigilance should, finally, go hand in hand with Dutch support for and encouragement of those social elements least under the sway of Islamic fanaticism, the *adat* chiefs and rulers of the Outer Islands and the traditional aristocracy on Java. In the process, he provided the analytical grounding of a policy that would twin religious tolerance toward those who acquiesced in Dutch rule with a brutal counterinsurgency targeting those who did not.[88] It may be said that Hurgronje pioneered the policy of distinguishing "Europe's 'good Muslims' " from its Muslim political adversaries.[89]

So what would religious tolerance mean in practice when it came to religious law regulating day-to-day behavior? Hurgronje had no doubt that tolerance would need to be framed by relations of power ensuring the supremacy of *adat* over religious law under the leadership of *adat* chiefs: "*adat* (custom law) and *hukom* (religious law) should take their places side by side in a good Mohammedan country," indeed, "in such a way that a very great portion of their lives is governed by *adat* and only a small portion by *hukom*."[90]

Hurgronje's trailblazing work paved the way for Professor Cornelis Van Vollenhoven (1874–1933) to later transform the study of *adat* law itself into a disciplinary "science." Christiaan Snouck Hurgronje and Cornelis Van Vollenhoven were the pioneers of indirect rule in the Dutch East Indies. Cornelis Van Vollenhoven built on the legacy of Christiaan Snouck Hurgronje. Vollenhoven joined the battle in 1904 when the Minister of Colonies, Idenberg, introduced a bill aimed at unifying the law for all inhabitants of the East Indies ("Europeans," "natives," and "foreign Orientals"). Against the dominant assumption that Dutch civilizing influence in the Indies must lead to the Westernization of law, Vollenhoven advocated legal pluralism. Gazetted in 1906, the bill was subsequently amended but never implemented as *adat;* it remained the focus of legal debates in the colony. Vollenhoven arrived in Indonesia in 1907 and spent a lifetime codifying *adat* law *(adatrecht)*. Van Vollenhoven invented the word *adatrecht* "but only after he had tried other terms, such as "Oriental popular law," in his effort to differentiate between Western law and "Oriental legal institutions."[91]

The Dutch created the concept of *hukom adat*. Before Van Vollenhoven and his school began codifying what to Western jurists appeared to be the juridical aspects of native custom, *adat* law was not a separate, independent entity, but an integral part of a history, a mythology, and an institutional landscape. Von Vollenhoven was clear as to the purpose of the project, he called *adatrecht:* "Our objective is not to know *adat* law for the sake of juridical science, still less to impede Indonesia's development by fondly preserving *adat*-curiosa; our aim is to create, not on paper but in reality, good government and a good administration of justice, both of which are unthinkable without a thorough knowledge of indigenous law and indigenous conceptions."[92] To understand the full significance of *adatrecht*, we need to see it as a political project.

Snouck Hurgronje went on to advise the French government on the subject of codifying Berber customary law in 1931, the year that he presided over the International Congress of Orientalists in Leiden. As in Indonesia, where Von Vollenhoven had given the practical finish to the project Hurgronje had conceived, Jacques Berque completed the project of implementing Berber customary law in Morocco.[93]

As with Maine, Hurgronje, too, saw external historical influences as so many impurities—never mind prevailing notions of progress in the West—and was determined to take as many steps back in history as necessary to disentangle the external from the internal in the name of, first, defining and then restoring and preserving tradition. Eventually, the Indies came to be administered through separate legal codes for Europeans, foreign Orientals, and natives; it was a system that was to remain in place until the Republic of Indonesia declared its independence in 1945.

As with the British in post-1857 India, the Dutch had advanced imperial strategy a step beyond the famed Roman practice of "divide and rule." The theorists of indirect rule—Henry Maine and Christiaan Snouck Hurgronje—did not play geopolitics as a game of set pieces. They no longer accepted boundaries or authorities or even popular subjectivities as unalterable givens. As we shall see with the colonies of twentieth-century Africa, they aimed at renegotiating everything—boundary, authority, and subjectivity. They shifted focus from existing elites—set pieces—to the population as a whole. The architects of indirect rule had vast ambitions: to remake subjectivities so as to realign its bearers. This was no longer just divide and rule. It was define and rule.

....

CHAPTER TWO

Nativism: The Practice

What is the significance of Sir Henry Maine today? In a book that came out after I gave the Du Bois lectures,[1] Karuna Mantena locates Maine in the flow of modern Western thought and shows the ways in which he was central to a reformulated justification of colonial rule following the mid-nineteenth century crisis of empire. It is this reformulated justification, this discourse, that Mantena terms "alibi." I share Mantena's interest in Maine as the theoretician of indirect rule. But I have two additional interests: one is to understand the practice of indirect rule as a form of what Michel Foucault called "governmentality"; the other is the theoretical and practical response of the colonized to colonial power, both the former response from scholars and the latter from practitioners of statecraft.

Maine's significance lies less in this "alibi"—his evolutionary theory of law and political forms (which he was not the first to formulate)—than in the fact that he was the originator of a new and modern technology of rule. Indirect rule was about the understanding and management of difference. From Maine's point of view, 1857 testified to the crisis of direct rule, the civilizing mission and its project of assimilation aimed at colonized elites. The classic example of this assimilationist project was the Roman Empire, which was after all the declared model for the British as well as the French. Unlike direct rule, indirect rule aimed at the reproduction of difference as custom, not its eradication as barbarism. It focused on ordinary people, not just the colonized elite. Before managing difference, colonial power set about defining it. Nick Dirks called this "the ethnographic state," which wielded the census not only as a way of acknowledging difference but also as a way of shaping, sometimes even creating, difference. The focus of colonial power, after 1857, was to define colonial subjectivity. Thus I have titled this book: *Define and Rule*.

The practice of indirect rule involved a shift in language, from that of exclusion (civilized, not civilized) to one of inclusion (cultural difference). The language of pluralism and difference is born in and of the colonial experience. Law is central to the project that seeks to manage and reproduce difference. The identities of colonized societies are not simply consensual (traditional), they are also enforced from above, through law. At the same time, law is not external to consensus; it participates in shaping it. Key to understanding the form of governmentality pioneered by Maine is the relationship between law and subjectivity.

Direct and indirect rule were not two consecutive phases in the development of colonial governance. Though the accent shifted from direct to indirect rule, the two continued in tandem: the civilizing mission (assimilation) existed alongside the management of difference (pluralism). The language of the civilizing mission shifted from the evangelical to the secular; its practice shifted from religious conversion to spreading the rule of law. And yet, claims of civil law as the universal marker of civilization went alongside recognition of different systems of customary law. The combination gave rise to regimes of legal hybridity, to legal pluralism, and to the question: what is law and what is custom? What do we mean by customary law?

I argued in Chapter 1 that if direct rule aimed to assimilate elite groups through a civilizing mission, the ambition of indirect rule was to remake the subjectivities of entire populations. It endeavored to shape the present, past, and future of the colonized by casting each in a nativist mold, the present through a set of identities in the census, the past through the driving force of a new historiography, and the future through a legal and administrative project.[2] Through this triple endeavor, the colonial state created a system of state-enforced internal discrimination—for which it claimed the mantle of tradition— thereby effectively fragmenting the colonized majority into so many administratively driven political minorities. In Africa, this political minority was called the tribe.

What is tribe? In what form did it exist before colonialism? How was it shaped by the political project of the colonial state? This is the main question I intend to ask in this chapter.

The modern state endeavors to stand up to time. Thus it

seeks to give itself a past and a future. If the production of the past is the stuff of history writing, the securing of a future is the domain of law making. Between the two, there is a strategic alliance: law identifies agency in the present and in history. By enforcing group identities on individual subjects, the law institutionalizes group life. A representation of how law maps group life can be found in the census. In post-1857 India, the law enforced, the census recorded and history memorialized three group-based political identities among the colonized: caste, religion, and tribe. In post-Berlin Conference African colonies, group life revolved around two politicized identities: race and tribe.

RACE AND TRIBE

To understand how political identities may be defined through the force of law, let us take an African example from an indirect rule colony in the first half of the twentieth century. In most African colonies, the census classified the population into two broad, overall groups: one called *race*, the other *tribe*. The distinction between race and tribe provides us a clue to the technology of colonial governance. I will highlight the ways in which the race-tribe distinction was key to governance through four related observations based on a reading of the census in different twentieth-century African colonies.

First, the census divided the population into two kinds of groups; some were tagged as races and others as tribes. When

46

a census-taker entered your name, it was either as member of a race or as member of a tribe. What determined whether you belonged to a race or a tribe? The distinction was not between colonizer and colonized, but between native and non-native. *Non-natives* were tagged as *races*, whereas *natives* were said to belong to *tribes*. *Races* were said to comprise all those officially categorized as not indigenous to Africa, whether they were indisputably foreign (Europeans, Asians) or whether their foreignness was the result of an official designation (Arabs, Colored, Tutsi). *Tribes*, in contrast, were all those defined as indigenous in origin. Rather than highlight the distinction between colonizers and colonized, the race-tribe distinction cut through the single category—colonized—by politically distinguishing those indigenous from those foreign. When the state officially distinguished nonindigenous races from indigenous tribes, it paid heed to one single characteristic, *origin*, and totally disregarded all subsequent developments, including, *residence*. By obscuring an entire history of migrations, the state portrayed the native as the product of geography rather than history.

Second, the race-tribe distinction had a direct legal significance. Whether a person was defined as belonging to a race or a tribe determined the law under which that person would live. All *races* were governed under a single law: civil law. This, however, was not true of tribes and the law under which they were governed: customary law. There was never a single customary law to govern all tribes as natives, as one racialized group. Each *tribe* was ruled under a separate set of laws; there were thus as many sets of customary laws as there were said to be tribes. It was said that tradition was tribal, why natives must be acknowledged first and foremost as belonging to separate tribes, with each tribe governed by a law reflecting its own tradition. Yet most would agree that the cultural difference between races—such as whites and Asians—was greater than that between tribes. To begin with, different races spoke different languages, mutually unintelligible. Often, they practiced different religions. They also came from different parts of the world, each with its own historical archive. No matter how different they were, tribes were neighbors and usually spoke languages that were mutually intelligible; they also claimed histories that were at times shared, at other times overlapping.

My point is simple: even if *races* were as different culturally as whites, Asians, and Arabs, they were ruled under a single, imported European law—called civil law—modified to suit a colonial context. Even if their languages were similar and mutually intelligible, *tribes* were governed under separate laws, called "customary" laws, which were in turn administered by ethnically defined native authorities. With *races*, the cultural difference was not translated into separate legal systems. Instead, it was contained, even negotiated, within a single legal system and was enforced by a single administrative authority. But with *tribes*, the case was the opposite: cultural difference was reinforced, exaggerated, and built up into different legal systems, each enforced by a separate administrative and political authority. In a nutshell, different races were meant to have a common future; different tribes were not. The colonial legal project—civil and customary—was an integral part of the colonial political project.

My third observation: the two legal systems were entirely different in orientation. To understand the difference, one only needs to contrast English common law with colonial customary law. English common law was presumed to change with circumstances. It claimed to recognize different interests and interpretations. But customary law in the colonies assumed the opposite. It assumed that law must not change with changing circumstances. Rather, any change was considered *prima facia* evidence of corruption. Both the laws and the enforcing authorities were called "traditional." Colonial powers were concerned first and foremost with establishing the credentials of their native allies as traditional and authentic. They were preoccupied with defining, locating, and anointing the traditional authority—in the singular. We need to remember that African colonies did not share with early modern Europe the political history of an absolutist state. This means that the rule-making authority was not in the singular but always plural. Instead of a centralized state authority whose writ was law—in all social domains—the practice was for different authorities to define the convention in different domains of social life. Besides chiefs, the definers of tradition could come from women's groups, age groups, clans, religious groups, and so on.

49

Once a single authority, called the chief, was exalted as *the* traditional authority, it was a short step to define tradition, too, as single, noncontradictory, and authoritative.[3] Marked by two characteristics, age and gender, the authority of the chief was inevitably patriarchal. With its "indirect rule" allies ensconced as "customary," the colonial state became both the custodian and the enforcer of tradition. Enforcing tradition became a way of entrenching colonial power. The fact is that colonial powers were the first political fundamentalists of the modern period. They were the first to advance and put into practice two propositions: one, that every colonized group has an original and pure tradition, whether religious or ethnic; and two, that every colonized group must be made to return to that original condition, and that the return must be enforced by law. Put together, these two propositions constitute the basic platform of every political fundamentalism in the colonial and the postcolonial world.

Fourth, by institutionalizing discrimination in colonial society—racial in civil law and tribal in customary law—civil and customary law reproduced a double division among the colonized. By joining the language of rights to that of civilization, civil law created a hierarchy of rights as an entitlement of different races said to occupy different positions on the civilizational ladder. It not only distinguished between the colonizing *master race* (Europeans) and colonized *subject races* (Asians, Arabs, Colored, and so on) and discriminated in favor of the former and against the latter, it also split the colonized population into two groups privileging non-native subject races in relation to native tribes.

If the first legally sanctioned division among the colonized was racial, the second was tribal: customary law, in turn, distinguished between two kinds of tribes and tribespersons, native and non-native. It grounded rights—and thus discrimination—in a discourse on origin (nativism). Unlike race, which claimed to mark a civilizational hierarchy, tribe was said to be a marker of cultural diversity. Natives were said to be tribal by nature and the practice of governing them was called native administration. At the heart of native administration was an administrative distinction between native and non-native tribes. Non-natives were identified as such no matter how many generations they had lived in the area, for no amount of time could erase the difference in origin. Every colony was divided into so many tribal homelands, each homeland identified with a tribe administratively tagged as native. Immigrants wanting access to land could only do so as "strangers" who had to pay a specified tribute to chiefs in the native authority. Colonial customary law acknowledged only one form of stable land tenure: the customary right of use [not ownership] in the tribal homeland.

The native identity involved three distinct privileges. The first was right of access to land. The second involved right of participation in the administration of the native authority. Chiefs in the native authority could only be appointed from among those identified as natives. It was only at the lowest level

of administration—the lowest tier of the native authority—
that one could find village headmen from resident non-native
tribes in a tribal homeland. The higher the level of native
authority, the stricter was the observance of the colonially
sanctioned custom that only natives have the right of representation and governance in the homeland. The third privilege
was in the area of dispute settlement, for every native authority
settled disputes on the basis of customary laws that privileged
natives.

The institutionalized regime of inequality between sup-
posedly original residents and subsequent immigrants led to a
monoethnic administration ruling over a multiethnic society.
With all key rights—from access to land to participation in
local governance to rules for settling local disputes—defined
as group rights and declared the privilege of members of the
native tribe, it was only a matter of time and circumstance
before an explosive confrontation developed between two
kinds of residents in every native authority: those defined as
native and those not. A monotribal administration overseeing
a triple tribal monopoly—over land, governance, and dispute
settlement—institutionalized tribal discrimination.

Although tribal identity in many cases coincided with what
anthropologists call ethnic identity—by which they usually
mean language-based, cultural, identity—this was not always
the case. In some cases, the same ethnic group was divided into
several tribes administratively. In other cases, tribes were designated arbitrarily—"invented," it is said in the literature.[4] The

only commonality between all these cases is that during the colonial period tribe was everywhere an administrative unit and tribal identity an officially designated administrative identity. For this reason, I believe it is best to refer to the system of native administration and indirect rule as a system that institutionalized tribal discrimination and justified it as an inevitable consequence of cultural identity. It thereby reified cultural identity into an administratively driven political identity, or ethnicity into tribe.

HISTORIOGRAPHY

There are two kinds of colonial histories. The grand narrative of colonialism, its meta-history, is written in bold within the frame of race. Its micro-histories are written in small script within the frame of tribe. Race was said to represent historical progress, culminating in the development of the state. The development from tribe to race was taken to represent a world historical shift in the basis of association, from kin group to locality (territory)—as portrayed in Barthold Georg Niebuhr's three-volume *History of Rome*.[5] Tribe and state are seen as two contrasting forms of association, the former nonterritorial, the latter territorial. Maine, we have seen, argued that, when it comes to tribes, political relations are articulated through the kinship principle.[6]

The racialized historiography of Africa was written in the nineteenth century. It has a name: the Hamitic Hypothesis.

These histories also have an unmistakable moral: that Africa was civilized from the outside, with light-skinned or fine-featured migrants from the north civilizing natives to the south. The Hamitic Hypothesis has several versions: colonial and nationalist. The standard regional histories are those of Central and West Africa. Nineteenth- and early twentieth-century colonial versions of central African history that cast the Tutsi as the Hamites and the Hutu as the natives can be read not only in the writings of the explorer John Hennings Speke[7] and those of the Church Fathers,[8] but also in those of the Rwandese Tutsi historian, Alexis Kagame.[9] In West African history, the Berbers were cast in the role of Hamites and were presented as the founders of Hausa states and thus civilizers of the Hausa. In this version of history, seminally critiqued by Abdullahi Smith,[10] who founded the Department of History at Ahmadu Bello University in Zaria, Nigeria, the Fulani appeared as the West African counterpart of the Tutsi in East Africa. Yet a third regional version can be found in the widespread historiographical notion of "Arabization," which provided the conceptual thread that knit together disparate histories of the Sudan. An influential Pan-Africanist version of the Hamitic Hypothesis came from the pen of Cheikh Anta Diop, who cast Egypt as the great civilizer of the rest of Africa. When Cheikh Anta cast Egyptians of the Pharaohnic period as a black people, he darkened the complexion of Hamites but left the logic of colonial historiography intact.

In the colonial version, racialized histories were narrated in an assimilationist mode; in contrast, tribalized histories were cast in a segregationist frame. Their overall point was to underline the progressive nature of race, which would inevitably break through the isolationist and inward-looking impulse identified with tribe. I shall illustrate the assimilationist paradigm with reference to two historical polities: the sultanates of Sennar and Dar Fur from northern Sudan. The conventional history of both sultanates—as of northern Sudan—is written as that of "Arabization."

Arabization refers to the spread of Arabic language (and, in general, culture) and genealogy.[11] The dominant historiography, both colonial and nationalist, assumes that Arabization was the result of Arab immigration from outside Sudan. This historiography has its roots in the colonial period. Its general outlines can be glimpsed in the journalistic writing of the young Winston Churchill who came to celebrate Kitchener's reclamation of Sudan from the Mahdiyya at the turn of the century. In *The River War*,[12] Churchill wrote of Sudan as a place where Arab settlers had subjugated and subordinated native Negro tribes. The scholarly elaboration of this theme can be found in the two-volume *History of the Arabs in Sudan* written by Harold MacMichael, a colonial administrator, in 1922.[13] The first volume focused on Negroes and Hamites, said to be the tribes resident in Sudan before the Arab migration and thus characterized as native. The second volume provided an account of Arab migration. It was a story that combined two features: the genealogy of individual Arab tribes and the migration of Arabs as a race. Though MacMichael recognized that the genealogies were constructed and were sometimes pure invention, he presented them as so many pieces of a jigsaw puzzle illustrating a single story of migration.

This colonial historiography was embraced in its outlines by nationalist historians, the most outstanding of them being Yusuf Fadl Hasan at the University of Khartoum. A contemporary version can be found in Ali Mazrui's account of Afrabia.[14] The colonial-nationalist historiography portrayed Sudan as a virgin land covered with layers of successive external influences. This land with one of the longest continuous written historical records was depicted as a place so lacking in internal dynamics that any significant impulse for change was said to come from the outside. Its six-millennia-long written history was periodized into successive epochs, each named to highlight a different external influence: Pharaohnic, Christian, Arab-Islamic, and Western. In every case, Arabization was presented as a civilizing mission. In writing a derivative history, nationalists reaffirmed the racialized historiography of Sudan as written in the colonial period—as an account of an ongoing confrontation of natives against settlers, the former Negroes and the latter Arabs.

We can piece together an alternative historiography from writings of a number of archaeologists, political scientists, and anthropologists. These scholars came from a generation that was strongly influenced by the anticolonial and antiwar movements of the 1960s and 1970s.[15] Critical of the ideological notion that the history of Africa was made from the outside and by lighter-skinned Hamites, as well as of the methodological tendency to privilege migration at the expense of internal developments, they looked for a more convincing explanation of the interaction between external influences and internal developments, one that would be based on the decisive role of internal factors in shaping the effect of outside influences.

The alternative explanation for Arabization—for the spread of Arabic culture and identity—lies in the history of state formation. Immigration by itself did not spread Arabic culture or identity. When Arab refugees first entered Nubia and Beja, observers noted a process of de-Arabization: Arab immigrants not only adopted the Nubi and Beja languages (and ceased to speak Arabic), they also gave up their nomadic lifestyle for an agricultural one. It is the state that drove the program of Arabization, but that state did not have to be the result of Arab conquest. For starters, we need to acknowledge that there was never an Arab invasion of Sudan. The invasion that did take place was that of the dynasty of Mamluks, a slave dynasty in Egypt, pursuing Arabs who had entered Sudan as refugees from southern Egypt.

The interesting fact is that the process of Arabization was the strongest, not in Nubia and Beja, the target of the invasion, but in the sultanate of Funj, where there was no invasion. The period from the time the sultanate was founded—in early sixteenth century—to colonization in the nineteenth century witnessed Arabization in three different phases: in the first period, the Funj royalty, which, according to all evidence, was of local southern Shilluk origin, claimed Arab descent. Take, for example, the testimony of the well-known Jewish adventurer David Reubeni, who visited Sudan in late 1522 and early 1523, spending ten months as a guest of the Sultan of Funj on the banks of the Blue Nile.[16] Having been told that the sultan claimed to be a descendent of the Prophet Muhammad, Reubeni, too, claimed a similar pedigree. According to Reubeni, the sultan would address him, thus: "What is it you desire of me, my lord, son of my Prophet?" To which Reubeni would customarily answer, "I love you and I give you my blessing . . . and the blessings of the Prophet Mohammed . . . and in another year I hope you will come to us in the city of Mecca, the place of the forgiveness of sins." It should not be surprising that both the king and the adventurer claimed holy descent. It was, after all, common for royal houses in the Sudanic belt in that era to claim descent from the lineage of prophets and holy men. The best-known example of this practice is the claim by the royal house of Ethiopia that its members were descended from King Solomon.

A process of mercantile development, which reached its height in the eighteenth century, ushered in the second phase in the history of Arabization. Jay Spaulding estimates that the number of towns in the Funj sultanate increased from only two in the early part of the eighteenth century to between twenty and thirty toward its end.[17] Centers of administration at the outset of the century, towns came to be dominated by merchants and *fuqara* (holy men) by the end of the century. The increase in the number of merchant towns was evidence of expanded trade and growing influence of the merchant population. As trade expanded, so did trade-based disputes. There then arose a conflict between merchants and royal power over the rules to be used to settle these new types of disputes. The royal house maintained that these disputes be settled by custom, but traders and the *fuqara* associated with them demanded that they be settled by the rules of *sharia*, known to be commerce-friendly. It is the conflict between custom and *sharia* that led the middle-class warlords (known as *Hamaj*) to confront and tame royal power and appoint regents to guide them. The merchants were as local as the royals. But, once victorious, merchants claimed Arab descent, an association with the House of the Prophet, and thus membership of the new commercial civilization: "We are Arabs."

The third period of Arabization took place in the colonial period, its high point coinciding with the growth and influence of anticolonial Pan-Arab movements, particularly Nasserism. If the Arab identity was limited to the royal house in the sixteenth century and afterward, and became a middle-class identity with the "Hamaj" revolution in the eighteenth century, it became a popular mass identity with the anticolonial movement in the twentieth century.

In historical Funj, the heartland of northern Sudan, Arab

came to be identified with settled peoples and with power, but such was not the case in Darfur, where Arab was an identity of nomads marginal to power. Unlike the Arabs of historical Funj, who were mainly sedentary, with only a sprinkling of nomads, Arabs of Darfur were among the nomadic tribes who had historically moved around the edges of the Sahara and lived on the margins of states that formed within the Saharawi ecological zone.

According to historians, the sultanate of Dar Fur was formed around 1650. Four institutions provided the foundation for this centralized authority and made possible its dominance over local land-based powers. These included a system of landed estates, Islam as a court religion, Arabic as a court language, and a newly developed standing army and administration. The sultans conferred two kinds of land grants on their subjects, one collective and the other individual. These grants were respectively called the administrative *hakura* and the *hakura* of privilege and were issued as written royal charters, many of which are still preserved at the museum in El Fasher in North Darfur. Whereas the collective grant was more likely a formal acknowledgement of land already held by communities, it is the grant of individual titles to court notables that was the really revolutionary departure in the development of land tenure in the sultanate. In time, the significance of individual tenure grew just as that of group tenure was progressively reduced. The grant of individual tenure went alongside the development of a royal bureaucracy: a royal appointee

60

to the provinces was known as *maqdum*. First appointed to pastoralist areas, the *maqdum* soon became a standard feature of the sultan's rule in peasant communities.

The practice of Islam as a court religion went alongside the use of Arabic as a language of state affairs. Islam in Dar Fur was organized in the form of Sufi brotherhoods *(tariqas)* and was strongly shaped by West African influence. There are records from as early as the eleventh century of West African pilgrims moving through Dar Fur on their way to the Haj in Mecca. Few at home expected pilgrims to return, which was why the departure ceremony for pilgrims was the same as the ceremony at funerals. Several additional impetuses during the nineteenth and twentieth centuries increased the flow of immigrants: the most important being the flight of refugees following the unsuccessful resistance to Western conquest in the nineteenth century, and flight from harsh forced labor practices in nearby French colonies in the twentieth century. Some, like the Fulani, came as groups and took on the identity of an Arab tribe—one of the tribes that make up the Southern Rizeigat—in South Darfur. O'Fahey, a historian of Dar Fur, estimated that by 1980 West African immigrants in Darfur may have comprised as much as 30 percent of the population of the province.[18]

The learned holy men of the Sufi brotherhoods, the *fuqara*, were one source from which the sultanate recruited members of the bureaucracy. The other—and probably more important source—was slaves. The weight of evidence on the slave trade suggests that the bulk of those enslaved remained in the sultanate; only a minority was sold in Egypt. Those who remained were mainly incorporated into the army. From the most ambitious and talented of the slaves—eunuchs—came royal slave-administrators, including the *maqdum*. O'Fahey says that so powerful were the royal slaves by the beginning of the nineteenth century that they were in a position to decide on the successor to the throne, which is why there were no battles over succession in Dar Fur after 1803. Ruled out as successors to the throne, the revenge of royal slaves was to become custodians who controlled succession to the throne.

In spite of its name, Dar Fur, the sultanate was not a tribal kingdom. As the kingdom grew, the Fur came to constitute a minority in its ethnic makeup. As the kingdom consolidated, the sultans moved the court outside the historical area of the Fur and established the capital at El Fasher in the north. The sultans were as local as their subjects, but, like many other royal houses of the time, they, too, claimed descent from Arab lineages. Prominent in the elite of the sultanate were three groups: court and army officials mainly recruited from royal slaves; the holy men *(fuqara)*, some from the Nile Valley, but most of West African origin; and traders who came mainly from the Nile Valley. It was an elite more cosmopolitan than parochial. It included two different groups of immigrants: forced migrants (slaves) from the south and free migrants from West Africa and the Nile Valley. Though the weight of Arab migration was small in Dar Fur, even less than in the sultanate of Funj, the significance of the process of Arabization was no less. Arabic was the language of the court, of commerce, of theology, and of education. The reason for this lay not in the facts of immigration but in the process of state and market formation.

Slavery and the slave trade were central to the process of state formation. In contrast with the market-driven character of modern slavery, premodern slavery was driven mainly by the demands of the state. It was the source of recruits for key organs of the state, from the army to the bureaucracy. The royal house needed to be independent of land-based interests. To build up a reliable army and officialdom, it needed a human resource independent of local clans and tribes. Loyalty was at a premium, and it was seen as a function of lack of attachments. For such a source of loyal soldiers and officials, the court turned to slaves. Forcibly separated from natal societies, the slave could be moved at will, whether from one locality to another or up and down the state hierarchy. The castrated slave—the eunuch—came to be the most extreme example of this lack of attachment and was prized as a highly desirable agent by those in positions of power and authority. Not only were royal slaves often castrated, the most ambitious of the slaves sometimes underwent castration in the hope of realizing ambition. In the kingdoms and empires of the precapitalist world, unlike in the plantations of the capitalist world, it was not unusual for some talented slaves to rise up the state hierarchy and be among the most powerful of state officials.

63

The title-holding hierarchy of Dar Fur—as of other Sudanic states—included persons of both slave and free origin. The best known of these was Muhammad Kurra, ex-officio governor of eastern Dar Fur under the sultan Muhammad Tayrab. The premodern royal slave was the quintessential public servant, with not even the possibility of a private attachment.

All evidence points to the conclusion that slavery in northern Sudan—in the Sultanates of Funj and Dar Fur—was not introduced from the outside. It developed as a local institution, alongside the development of centralized power in the two sultanates. Despite the expression "Arab slavery," we must be aware that the entry of non-Sudanese—both Europeans and Arabs—into the slave trade in Sudan really followed the extension of plantation slavery from the Caribbean to Indian Ocean islands in the late eighteenth century and the advent of Turco-Egyptian rule from Egypt to Sudan in the early nineteenth century—a fact that W. E. B. Du Bois stressed over and again in *Africa and the World*.

THE MAHDIYYA

In the history of British colonialism, the Mahdiyya must rank as second, after 1857 India, in the hierarchy of anti-imperialist movements that shook the very foundations of imperial rule, promoting a re-think of policy. If 1857 led to a re-think of the civilizing mission in India, the Mahdiyya led to an active transfer of the lessons of 1857 to Britain's African colonies, starting with Darfur. The Mahdiyya raised the specter of a trans-local, anti-colonial resistance; the colonial response to this was tribalization, a form of local governance that decentralized despotism.

The Turco-Egyptian colonization of northern Sudan lasted from 1821–1886. It destroyed or subordinated the old ruling elites. The only surviving institution with the potential to provide anchor for a countrywide resistance was the Sufi brotherhood. No surprise the brotherhoods were at the forefront of the resistance when it came. Militant Mahdism was an import from West Africa. The expectation of a messiah, a Mahdi, to coincide with the new Islamic millennium, had been widespread in the Sudanic belt.

The Sudanese Mahdiyya was a contradictory phenomenon, politically emancipatory but socially repressive. On the positive side, it was a broad anti-imperialist alliance of a multitude of ethnic groups against foreign occupation. It was the first time peoples of the West (Kordofan and Darfur) and those of the Nile had joined together in a single movement. More than any other movement, it was the Mahdiyya that forged the basis of a common northern Sudanese identity. In addition, the Mahdiyya, especially the army—often known as the Dervish—had strong links in the south of Sudan. The key components of the army were the cavalry and the riflemen. The Dervish cavalry was drawn by and large from the nomadic Baqqara, known to be fine horsemen or camel riders. The Ansar riflemen—the Jihadiya "armed with single-shot, .45 calibre Remington breech-loaders taken from their fallen opponents or from captured Egyptian arsenals"—usually came from the south, the Nuba Mountains, or the west.[19] In the course of the revolution, many of the *bazinger*—private armies recruited from the south by slave traders—joined the Mahdiyya, as did many from the government army.[20] The Mahdi died only a few months after the revolution succeeded and the state was established. The Khalifa, who succeeded the Mahdi, incorporated the Baqqara tribes of Darfur in the army and set up his own elite corps of bodyguards, the *mulazimin;* these fighters, too, were mostly southerners.[21] As a movement, the Mahdiyya drew its followers and cadres not only from the Arab north but also from the west (Darfur and Kordofan), the south and regions bordering it (the Nuba Mountains); it was the first to crisscross the north and the south, the east and the west, and Arab and non-Arab parts of Sudan. Many Sudanese in the anticolonial movement of succeeding decades rightly thought of the Mahdi as the father of the nation.

The Mahdiyya also unleashed brutal violence against those outside its ranks, evoking comparisons with the brutal violence of the slave raids. Though the Mahdi died only months after setting up a state, the violence continued through the rule of his deputy, the Khalifa Abdullah, born of an immigrant family from West Africa. From 1885 to 1888, there were a series of revolts against the Mahdist state from the Baqqara and the Fur, who had been among the staunchest supporters of the Mahdiyya. The Khalifa responded to the opposition with brutal violence, involving forced population transfers from southern Dar Fur to Kordofan and the Mahdist capital, Omdurman. In power for thirteen years, the Khalifa made it a policy to break the power of any tribal hierarchy that opposed him. Such was the fate of the Kabbabish and the Beja; stripped of livestock, both were impoverished and subordinated by the centralized Mahdist state. Due to extreme violence combined with widespread famine and devastating epidemics, it is estimated that nearly a third of the population of northern Sudan perished over the two decades that spanned Mahdist victory and rule and subsequent British conquest. Though most of the English-language scholarship on the Mahdiyya has been colored by unsympathetic British sources, recent sources have tended to acknowledge that the Mahdiyya commanded broad support from the Sudanese population. "The Mahdist Sudan was not a total tyranny, in spite of British attempts to present it as such. The Khalifa Abdulla ruled firmly but fairly according to his rights and the Sudanese people were perfectly content under his rule, certainly far happier than they had been under the Egyptians, and but for the return of the British army in the 1890s, the Mahdist state would in all likelihood have continued and prospered."[22]

The Mahdiyya was similar to a number of anti-imperialist movements in early twentieth-century Africa. All faced a seemingly insurmountable problem, one of scale. The big question was how to forge a translocal movement against the transnational forces of the empire. That question was solved in several places in similar ways: the common thread was the binding influence of a spiritual ideology as developed in the Maji Maji resistance in Tanganyika or the Shona resistance in Rhodesia. As John Iliffe noted of the Maji Maji: "The central figure in such an enlargement was the prophet, proclaiming a new religion in order to supersede the old, a new loyalty to transcend old loyalties of tribe and kinship."[23] The holy water the prophet offered, the *maji*, not only provided assurances of impunity against the white man's firepower, it also made for a lasting bond between those who accepted it. The Maji Maji terrified those of its German adversaries who glimpsed in it signs of an imminent political transformation.

The Mahdiyya was the largest of the resistance movements of the period, certainly the largest since the 1857 uprising in India, and it shook the foundations of empire to the core—not just in Istanbul, but also in Paris and London. *The Times* (London) of February 6, 1885, noted: "The shock caused by the news of the fall of Khartoum has no parallel in the experience of the present generation." "Our power in the East will be ruined," the queen wrote to a confidant, "We shall never be able to hold up our heads again." The Liberal prime minister, Gladstone, otherwise known to be a strong opponent of imperial expansion, took care to cover his right flank and told his cabinet that Britain must not ignore "the effect which the triumph of the Mahdi would have on our Mahometan subjects."

With nothing less than the survival of British India at stake, the cabinet decided it must avenge Gordon.[24]

That revenge was a devastating victory won by forces under General Kitchener on the plains a few miles from the Mahdist capital at Omdurman. Though the Battle of Omdurman took place at the Khalifa's initiative, his ranks were bitterly divided, and the result was a total disaster for the Mahdiyya.[25] The Dervishes were estimated to have lost more than twenty-six-thousand men killed and wounded at Omdurman, a staggering loss.[26] Kitchener's losses were minimal: just forty-eight men killed and eighty-two wounded. How are we to understand this lopsided outcome? G. W. Stevens, one of the British war correspondents, summed up the Mahdist achievement: "Our men were perfect, but the Dervishes were superb beyond perfection. It was the largest, best and bravest army that ever fought against us for Mahdism and it died worthy of the huge empire that Mahdism won and kept so long." A recent account of the war concludes: "If the estimates of the Kalifa's forces are correct, this represents a casualty rate of around fifty per cent—a tribute to the courage of the Ansar and evidence of the terrible effect of modern weapons when used against mass formations."[27] The Battle of Omdurman was testimony to more than just the unequal contest between anticolonial insurgency and colonial counterinsurgency in the modern era; it also spoke volumes of the savagery of which the forces were capable when challenged. That the Mahdist forces observed conventions of colonial warfare was not unconnected to its tragic outcome.

If most of the Ansar fought in spite of the certainty that the outcome would be death and defeat, why did the English forces, with such overwhelming odds in their favor, continue to dish out death and destruction? Observers had several explanations for this savagery. First, a certainty that loss would mean certain death: "the British troops who shot so efficiently were only too aware that they were shooting for their lives." But why kill to the finish? Why leave the wounded to die? "The battle left some sixteen thousand Dervish wounded, many now dead or still dying out in the desert and in the town."[28] To self-preservation, we must add another motive: total de-humanization of the adversary. Churchill reported that many in the army were so fueled with sentiments of revenge that, egged on by the strident British press, they came to regard the Ansar as "vermin—unfit to live": "I must personally record that there was a very general impression that the fewer the prisoners, the greater would be the satisfaction of the commander."[29]

Kitchener himself shared this thirst for revenge. In the short time between victory at Omdurman and having to leave to face the French commander at Fashoda, Kitchener did all he could to eradicate the memory of the Mahdi. On September 6, he ordered the destruction of the Mahdi's tomb, so that his body may be exhumed and thrown into the Nile—a task supervised by Major W. S. Gordon, a nephew of the late general. Having separated the Mahdi's skull from the body, the younger Gordon decided to present it to Kitchener, so the victorious general may "mount it on a stand and use it as an inkpot."[30]

When the British conquered the Mahdiyya, they set up the Sultanate of Dar Fur as a British protectorate, more or less in the fashion of many of the princely states in India. When they did establish direct control over Darfur, they made it the centerpiece of their strategy in Sudan. The thrust of British policy in Darfur can be summed up in one word: tribalization. As a strategy of governance, tribalization was the kernel of native administration and indirect rule. It was intended as the antidote to Mahdism.

TRIBALIZING AS A POLITICAL STRATEGY

Key to native administration was an administrative distinction between "natives" and "strangers." Natives were said to be original to the area, and non-natives were identified as such no matter how many generations they had lived in the area. Darfur, the province, was parceled into a series of homelands, *dars*, each identified with a tribe administratively tagged as native. The *dar* was considered the homeland of its native tribe. Immigrants wanting access to land could only do so as "strangers" who had to pay a specified tribute to the native authority. With all African land tenure identified as tribal, all other forms of tenure, including the individual land holding introduced during the sultanate—the *hakura* of privilege—was rendered obsolete. The *hakura* system in contemporary Darfur is not a continuation of the land system in the days of the sultanate; rather, it dates from the time the British introduced the process of tribalization.

Though the nomenclature, *dar*, evoked customary usage, its meaning was subverted. Before, *dar* had multiple meanings, with home signifying one of several locations, starting with one's immediate dwelling and extending to several localities in a series of concentric circles. But now *dar* identified the colonial administrative unit as home. Home became the tribal territory—tribal homeland—where one's group was defined as native. Just the fact that it defined a person's access to land, to participation in governance, including preference in the very process of dispute settlement, turned the membership of the administratively defined *dar* into a truly meaningful identity. Though imposed from above, through colonial law and associated administrative measures, tribal identity became the basis of voluntary organization over time. Enforced from above, native identity begot a native agency.

Though I have described this system in the context of Darfur, it is obtained in all African contexts that I have studied, from Eastern Africa to Nigeria, from Sudan to South Africa. The one exception was Rwanda. The big difference between Sudan and Rwanda was that whereas in the case of Sudan, Britain joined a racialized historiography to a tribalized administration, land tenure, and dispute settlement; in the case of Rwanda all—the historiography and the land tenure system, local administration and dispute resolution—were racialized. Every institution privileged Tutsi over Hutu.

A distinctive feature also marked the colonial experience of Darfur. As implemented in Darfur, the native authority system institutionalized a system of inequality between peasant and pastoralist tribes. This legacy led to a triply layered society— peasants, semi-nomads, and nomads—and was to lead to disastrous consequences in time. The colonial state looked at the peasant/nomad distinction from a predominantly political perspective, one driven by the realization that it would be easier to control sedentary peoples. This is the main reason peasant tribes were granted homelands *(dars)* that more or less coincided with their areas of settlement at the time of colonization, but the diminished *dars* of the semi-nomadic cattle tribes (the Baqqara) of the south more or less coincided with their areas of settlement but did not always include all their grazing areas. In sharp contrast, the fully nomadic camel tribes (the *abbala*) of the north—who had no settled villages and moved around all year—received no *dars*.

Did tribe exist before colonialism? If we understand by tribe an ethnic group with a common language, it did. But tribe as an administrative entity that distinguishes between natives and non-natives and systematically discriminates in favor of the former and against the latter—defining access to land and participation in local governance and rules for settling disputes according to tribal identity—certainly did *not* exist before colonialism. One may ask: did race exist before racism? As differences in pigmentation, or in phenotype, it did. But as a fulcrum for group discrimination based on "race" difference, it did not. The consensus among contemporary scholars of race is that while race does not exist, racism—a system of discrimation,

73

legal or social, based on the perception or conviction that race is real—does exist. Like race, tribe became a single, exclusive, and total identity only with colonialism. Above all, tribe was a politically driven, modern—*totalizing*—identity.

As a totalizing identity, tribe was a subset of race. Each represented a language of privilege and discrimination. The colonial state was based on a double discrimination, racial and tribal. Racial discrimination was institutionalized in the central state, and tribal discrimination in the local substate. Race was said to be about a hierarchy of civilization, whereas tribe was said to reflect cultural (ethnic) diversity within a race. If the central state justified *discrimination against the native race on civilizational grounds*, the local state justified *discrimination in favor of the native tribe on grounds of origin and difference*.

COMPARING WITH THE ROMAN EMPIRE

The British thought of themselves as the modern successors to the Roman Empire. They claimed to be the bearers of a rule of law, which they saw as the heart of the colonial civilizing mission. In what ways did the British Empire resemble that of the Romans and in what ways were the two different?

"The empire of the Romans," Henry Maine wrote in *Lectures on the Early History of Institutions*, "for one reason alone, must be placed in a totally different class from the Oriental despotisms, ancient and modern, and even from the famous Athenian Empire. All these last were tax-taking empires, which exercised little or no interference in the customs of village-communities or tribes. But the Roman Empire, while it was a tax-taking, was also a legislating empire. It crushed out local customs, and substituted for them institutions of its own. Through its legislation alone it effected so great an interruption in the history of a large part of mankind, nor has it had any parallel except—and the comparison is very imperfect—the modern British Empire in India."[31] I have already argued that British and French ambitions to export their respective institutions to different parts of the empire, and in the process assimilate local elites, were short-lived. Faced with resistance from old elites and demands for equal citizenship from new ones, modern European empires moved from the logic of assimilation to one of segregation. Their ambition to spread civil law through the assimilation of new elites gave way to a customary pact with old elites. It is not the comparison between Rome and modern European empires, but rather the contrast between them that can instruct us in understanding the ways in which empires have changed in the era of the modern nation-state.

The Roman Republic expanded in two phases, first to Italy, and then overseas. The experience in Italy had a profound impact on the nature of Roman rule in the overseas provinces. Rome settled its citizens all over Italy and assured them self-government in local affairs. Their example familiarized diverse Italian communities with the Latin language and Roman institutions, just as it convinced local elites "that they would lose little in local autonomy and gain much in prestige, protection from Roman magistrates and even political power, if they could secure the status of citizens." When they were denied citizenship by Rome, Italian communities rose in revolt in 90 BC. In response, Rome conceded citizenship. By the time of Augustus, all the Italians came to be Romans.[32] From the third century BC, Rome enlarged her dominions beyond the seas. Rome governed through local oligarchies wherever they existed. The standard pattern was for Rome to leave local elites to control the people and in return provide effective protection for their liberty, by which Rome meant above all the protection of property rights.

The outstanding feature of Roman imperial rule was the "ideal of inclusiveness."[33] Romans made citizenship increasingly inclusive with time.[34] Roman citizenship was granted, first and foremost, to communities, and then to individuals. Over time, Rome opened up citizenship to both subject peoples and slaves. Beginning with some of their Latin neighbors in the fifth century BCE, Rome decided after the 90 BCE revolt to enfranchise entire Italian communities.[35] Eventually, Emperor Caracalla granted citizenship to all the inhabitants of the Roman world in 212 CE.[36] Rome became multicultural. In spite of its name, the empire was less and less Roman. In the third century most senators were not Italians. From Trajan onward, most emperors came from the provinces. The eternal city celebrated its millennium in AD 247 under the rule of an Arab sheikh.[37]

Rome was also willing to grant citizenship to freed male slaves; only criminal slaves were totally debarred from citizenship. So prevalent was the practice of granting citizenship to slaves that Romans became concerned "with foreigners who fraudulently took on the status of slaves for a short time in order to use manumission as a route into Roman citizenship." The more it became universal, the less Roman citizenship carried with it equal rights under the law. On the one hand, "the upper classes were privileged, enjoying a sort of benefit of clergy." On the other hand, the status of a citizen ex-slave carried "some political and legal disadvantages."[38] It also debased the position of a Roman woman who, though she could give the right to vote to her male slave, could not vote herself.

There were two different kinds of Roman communities in the empire. The first were the colonies (*coloniae*), which were usually towns of ex-soldiers who became Roman citizens. Demobilized auxiliary soldiers received the right to obtain Roman citizenship for themselves, their wives and children after their discharge.[39] The constitution and laws of the colonies were entirely Roman. Like towns in Italy, they were freed from direct taxation.[40]

Whereas colonies were found in the east, municipalities (*municipia*) were more a feature of the west. The municipality could have either Roman or Latin status. Roman status indicated communities of Roman citizens; in contrast, Latin status signified a midway position of preexisting communities where Roman law held sway, and where only ex-magistrates—and in rare instances all town councilors—received the privilege of Roman citizenship. Latin rights were limited to the private rights of a Roman citizen—including intermarriage with Romans, inheritance from them, and the right to own Roman land—but not political right, except for symbolic participation in Roman assemblies when present in Rome.[41] This was how Adrian Sherwin-White summarized the main development: "It was as communities and not as individuals that the Italian allies were eventually incorporated in the Roman state, under the various enabling laws. . . . When they ceased to be states, they became self-governing *municipia*."[42]

If asked about the mechanism through which Rome held together an empire of more than fifty million, the answer would be simple: citizenship of different kinds, Roman citizens with full rights, and Latin citizens with partial rights, both linking the provinces to Rome.[43] But this did not exhaust the bill, for the majority of Greek cities remained communities with their own constitutions and local government.[44]

The big difference between the eastern and the western parts of the empire was that Romans tended to settle the west with colonies of soldiers, but to govern the east in alliance with local elites.[45] The remarkable fact was that no troops were needed to hold down the cities in the east because the most powerful of the local citizens, men to whom Rome had granted equality of rights, kept order and ensured loyalty. It is worth noting the well-known Panegyric on Rome from Aelius Aristides, the son of a landowner in the east who had received Roman citizenship, that the Roman Empire was the first that rested on consent and not on force. In the West, citizenship was far more widely diffused. Not only did whole communities possess it in several instances, more individuals could win it as a reward for military service, since over two thirds of the Roman army was raised and stationed in the western provinces.[46]

To these generalizations there was one notable exception, that of Judaea in the east. Whereas normal Roman practice was to hand over control in the eastern provinces "to a selected scion of the native dynasty," Herod's appointment by the Roman Senate as the King of Judaea following the conquest of Jerusalem in 37 by Roman legions began a new era, one that marked a breach in this policy.[47] "In marked contrast to the general freedom from Roman interference enjoyed by the Jewish population before the war," Jerusalem after 70 "became an occupied city."[48] The resistance to Roman rule was particularly fierce in Judaea, a fact that many writers attribute to the ideological element, being the role of religion in mobilizing Jewish opposition to Rome.[49]

Romans made two claims for the empire: one, that it provided security; and two, that it championed *humanitas*. Rome provided security in the provinces for at least six centuries, an outstanding record.[50] Its claim to being the custodian of *humanitas* in many ways resembles contemporary Western claims to being beacons of civilization. As "a guiding principle in human relations," one underlining "the concern of a master for a slave and of rulers for their subjects," the notion of "humanity" was developed by the Stoics. By the late first century BC, however, *humanitas* had been formulated as a thoroughly Roman concept. It is in this spirit that Cicero instructed his brother that "if fate had given you authority over Africans or Spaniards or Gauls, wild and barbarous nations, you would still owe it to your *humanitas* to be concerned about their comforts, their needs and their safety."[51]

Cicero's injunction makes clear that Romans came to formulate *humanitas* "as a qualification for rule." Though *humanitas* "was believed to have been invented only once," by Greeks, Romans claimed to be responsible for spreading *humanitas* throughout the world. In this sense, Romans stood as custodians of historical progress. As a claim, *humanitas* was central to the propagation of Roman power and to its legitimation.[52]

Humanitas was the lead term in the binary whose subordinate term was *barbarian*. Greeks conceptualized barbarians as the antithesis of Hellenes, which they defined not merely as those who spoke Greek and behaved like Greeks, but as a people descended from a common stock. Defined in cultural and biological terms, barbarians were natural slaves (Aristotle), they were morally underdeveloped. Romans adopted much of this definition of barbarism—strange languages, bizarre behavior, and moral inferiority—but common descent was not an issue with Romans. Whereas for Greeks the barrier with barbarians was "clear-cut and difficult to cross," Romans thought of it as "a continuum along which it was relatively easy to progress."

In contrast with the strongly segregationist Greek impulse, *humanitas* defined the more assimilationist Roman vision.[53]

Contemporary scholars have internalized the Roman claim to being the pioneers and custodians of progress—*humanitas*—by presenting the relationship between local communities and Roman power as one of cultural change, described as "Romanization." The concept assumes a linear relationship between political power and cultural change. Even in contexts where conquest has provided the stimulus to cultural change, the conqueror's culture has not always been the dominant one. Numerous examples testify to this: among these are the influence of Hellenistic culture on the Romans as they extended their power over the Greek world; the expansion of Han culture in China even when it was conquered, first by the Mongols and later by the Manchus, both of whom were Sinicized;[54] the spread of Farsi language and culture under the rule of Moghuls (otherwise ethnic Turks) in India; the spread of Sanskritic culture in India under British rule; and, finally, the spread of Arabic script and language under the non-Arab sultanates of Dar Fur and Funj in Sudan.

The problems with terms like Romanization—or Arabization—which claim to describe a process of cultural transformation, are several. By naming only one party in the process—Roman or Arabic—it "implies a unilateral downloading of a pre-packaged culture rather than a process of mutual adaptation in a wide variety of manners" and presents it as "the imposition of a superior Roman [or Arabic, for that matter] culture upon an inferior native one." An alternative perspective would see the local not "as objects or recipients" in a one-way process but as human actors with "not only knowledge and ability, but volition." One is reminded of Leopold Sedar Senghor's dictum to his people: Assimilate! Don't be assimilated! Romanization implies "a sudden, thorough and absolute process of assimilation." Instead of regarding locals and Romans as "separate, albeit interactive, entities involved in a two-way interchange," the alternative is to see both involved in a mutually transforming process. Because the final product partakes of both, no matter how unequally, and does not quite resemble either, the process is also identity-transforming for both sides. Not only did locals become provincials, Romans were also transformed. Classical sources, which obscure this process of identity transformation by presuming fixed identities at the beginning and the end of the process, are, in Curchin's phrase, guilty of "ethnic profiling."[55]

Among these scholars is Henry Maine who identified with empire builders and so admired Rome that he tended to forget some key differences between it and modern European colonial empires, particularly Britain.[56] To begin with, the longevity of the Roman Empire is striking. Peter Brunt reminds us that "in the provinces Rome first acquired her rule lasted for 600 years" whereas "less than 200 years separate Plassey from the grant of independence to India." His verdict is that "compared with Roman domination, the British was an ephemeral growth."[57] Second is the difference in how the two empires were organized. Not only was there no physical contiguity between modern European empires and their colonies, "the natives stayed in their own environment, and the colonies were never incorporated [in the motherland] in any real sense."[58] In contrast, the Roman Empire "grew by conquering and absorbing neighboring peoples, one after the other." The tendency was for the subjects in the colonies to lose their identity as peoples and for the elites to become Roman citizens.[59]

Unlike the Greek world and unlike modern Western empires, the Roman Empire tended to expand by "incorporating entire foreign communities in their body politic, whether as citizens with full rights or as citizens without the vote."[60] When provincial elites emulated Roman culture and demanded corresponding political rights, Rome did not rebuff them; it embraced them.[61] This is why, unlike with modern Western empires, those politically conscious in the Roman provinces were seldom disaffected. Brunt reminds us that "in the very century when Roman rule was to vanish in Gaul a Gallic poet celebrated Rome as the city which had unified the world by giving the conquered a share in rights" and then adds: "What a contrast with the jubilation that marks the independence days of British colonies!"[62] In the West at least, "Romans left behind them not memories of discontent but a continuing aspiration for European unity, and as Christianity took on a Roman coloring, for Christian unity."[63]

If there is a parallel to the Roman capacity to absorb local elites as the empire expanded—in the process turning Rome itself into a multicultural center—that parallel is provided by the Ottoman Empire and not by the modern Western empires of Britain or France. If there is a parallel with the British Empire, it is with the regime of direct rule in pre-1857 India when the Utilitarians aimed to anglicize and assimilate the Indian elite. In the century that followed 1857, the British Empire moved away from an elite-focused assimilationist policy to a mass-based culturalist policy. The point of that policy was less to civilize the elites than to shape popular subjectivities. In this sense, at least, the enterprise known as indirect rule was vastly more ambitious than what the Romans had imagined or practiced.

....

CHAPTER THREE

Beyond Settlers and Natives

The Theory and Practice
of Decolonization

Decolonization was the preoccupation of two groups that propelled the nationalist movement: the intelligentsia and the political class. They set out to create the nation, the former to give the independent state a history and the latter to create a common citizenship as the basis of national sovereignty. Both projects unraveled in the thick of civil war. It is time to ask: what have we learned? How far have we gone beyond settler claims to being custodians of cosmopolitan pluralism and nativist preoccupation with origin and authenticity?

THE INTELLECTUAL CRITIQUE

The shift from direct to indirect rule went alongside a number of changes. One of these was a change in the language of rule, from civilization to tradition. The local mediators of rule also changed: from educated strata to "traditional" chiefs. Direct rule had gone hand-in-hand with building Western-style schools and institutions of learning. A visible social sign of colonial rule was the proliferation of literate strata such as English-speaking lawyers. With the turn to indirect rule, colonial attitudes to the educated strata changed radically, from hope to suspicion.

The British brought to Africa an entire arsenal of lessons in colonial management drawn from nineteenth-century colonies such as India, Malaya, and the West Indies. Key British administrators in Africa, such as Lord Lugard, had more than likely served in the Indian Service. Lugard had been a former colonial official in India and Burma, then a fortune-seeking ivory hunter and merchant in equatorial Africa. Lugard later joined the Imperial British East Africa Company. As a pioneer of indirect rule, Lugard systematized its practice in Northern Nigeria and wrote about it in *The Dual Mandate*. He was determined that Nigeria must avoid "the Indian disease," by which he meant a native intelligentsia whose natural bent was to nationalist agitation.

The shift is best evident in the modern history of higher education in the colonies. In the eighteenth to mid-nineteenth centuries, a triumphant and confident empire placed high premium on civilizing the colonies. Universities had a pride of place in this mission. Challenged in mid-nineteenth century, the empire went on the defensive. As it opted for order over modernity, higher education ceased to be a priority. The shift was marked in places colonized last, such as the lands of Middle Africa, those between the Sahara and the Limpopo River, colonized in the aftermath of the Berlin Conference.

During the 1960s, the world media was full of stories of how one African colony after another was about to become independent, with no more than a handful of university graduates—Tanganyika, Congo, Nyasaland, Northern Rhodesia; the list was endless. Congo was said to have no more than nine university graduates at independence. "The British," complained independent Tanganyika's Prime Minister, Julius Nyerere, "ruled us for 43 years. When they left, there were two trained engineers and 12 doctors. This is the country we inherited."[1] The colonies of Middle Africa divided into two groups. Most had no universities at independence, which is why a national university—along with the national anthem, the national flag, and the national currency—became an obligatory sign of real independence. But a few had one university, usually a university meant to serve the region, such as Makerere University in Kampala, Uganda, or the University of Ibadan in Nigeria. At independence, in 1961, Nigeria had one university with a thousand students. In 1991, Nigeria had forty-one universities with 131,000 students. Nigeria was not an exception.[2] The African university was mainly a post-colonial development.

Nationalist governments built the developmentalist university. The more nationalism turned into a state-building project, the more pressures mounted on the developmental university to implement a state-determined agenda. Officialdom came to equate critical thought with a critique of nationalism and the nationalist elite. Indeed, the university occupied a contradictory location, for the university was an incubator of not only critical thought but also a political counter-elite. Critique could and did mask ambition. The more professors acted like ministers-in-waiting and, in some cases, like presidents-in-waiting, the more their critique sounded self-serving. In a single-party context, the university took on the character of an opposition party. Confrontations with governmental power often led to strikes and shutdowns.

Nationalists were seldom willing democrats. From George Washington to Indira Gandhi to Robert Mugabe—and we must also include among these the best of them, Nyerere and Nkrumah—they tended to see opposition as evidence of factionalism and betrayal. The postcolonial African university was a highly politicized institution. Sometimes, the politicization was at the expense of academic freedom and intellectual pursuits. To achieve a balance between relevance and scholarship would require an autonomous intellectual life, which in turn depended on putting sheer numbers of scholars in place and creating a significant density of institutional life. Among the few countries to afford these were Nigeria and South Africa. Not surprisingly, an alternative historiography to colonial conventions on race and tribe first developed in Nigeria.

I want to begin with a discussion of the writings of Yusuf Bala Usman, a historian at Ahmadu Bello University (ABU) in Zaria, Nigeria, and a towering figure among these postcolonial intellectuals. The last time I met Usman was in 2005 at ABU in Zaria. Usman suggested we meet in the evening around a few beers. I was surprised. "But you have Sharia law in the state now," I said. "Never mind, the university staff club is federal territory. State laws do not apply there." He was right. We had a wonderful evening of beers and roasted meat at the ABU Staff Club.[3]

At the time Usman wrote, historians of Africa were preoccupied with the question of historical sources. The debate among historians turned on the question of whether oral testimony could be as reliable a source of historical information as written texts. Just how defensive were the oral historians is clear from the remarks of one their doyens, Jan Vansina at the University of Wisconsin. To Usman's great disappointment, Vansina cautioned his colleagues that oral sources "need to be examined in terms of the world outlook which informs them" so these may be purged of "distortions" and "colourings" so they "merit(s) a certain amount of credence within certain limits." Usman wondered why such probing should stop with oral history. He wondered why the same critical approach "is not extended to the most widely used source of African history for the last five hundred years, namely the written records of European travelers, traders, missionaries, companies, governments and their agents."[4]

For Usman, all sources—not just oral, but also written— were subject to bias. But detecting the bias of sources was simply a first step in history writing. The more important question was how to detect and deal with one's own bias. That dilemma must face every historian for two reasons. To begin with, Usman was convinced that "establishing what happened at a particular place or time, no matter how much detail is known about it does not constitute the reconstruction of history." This is because "historical reconstruction requires a framework of explanation within which a series of events can be perceived and understood as a process."[5] History is written as a narrative, and the mode of the narrative—such as romance, tragedy, comedy, and farce—is not self-evident. It has to be chosen. Furthermore, there is the "very basic problem," one of "distance, detachment and objectivity," which must arise from "the relationship between the person making the study and the subject of study."[6] This is how Usman explained it:

> This is a fundamental problem in the physical, natural and human sciences. It is the problem which makes the study of history and society far more profound and complex than the study of physical and natural phenomena. The person with a perception of history who is studying history has been produced and moulded by history. The very concepts he uses are historically determined and produced. And he is involved in looking at what has produced and is moulding him. It is a much more complex and fundamental thing than the study of rocks and plants, for example. . . . Unfortunately, some of our colleagues in the study of society and history, impressed with the precision and quantification of the physical and natural sciences run

around and chase after what they regard as the prestige of these other sciences. As a result that, they give the impression that all you need is to develop better techniques and better computers, then you can reduce the study of history to the same level as the study of atoms. But in fact, they will find that no matter how fine the techniques they introduce, the phenomenological fact that you are studying yourself cannot be removed. You cannot relate to yourself as you relate to a donkey or a rock. You can't![7]

In other words, "there is no basis of 'objectivity' outside of history."[8] That, however, did not mean that one was locked into an impossible situation. The way out was to be conscious of the categories, conceptions, and assumptions that inform history-writing. The way out of the problem is to become conscious of the problem. Usman explained this in two steps: "It is . . . impossible to reconstruct history without having some specific categories, conception and assumption. What is suggested here is that unless this is done consciously one becomes a conceptual prisoner of certain types of primary sources, without being aware of it."[9] The second step was to recognize that one has no option but to look at the past from the vantage point of the present: ". . . since the purpose of historical study is to grasp the historical process for the purpose of influencing it then the only correct conceptual framework, for any epoch, is that which provides a basis for the practical determination of the direction of that epoch. . . . What I am saying is that every view you have of the past has specific implications regarding what you should do now."[10] A degree of self-reflexivity was necessary to write good history: "Once you are aware of your own historicity, then you will realize the historicity of the concepts that you use, and you do not sit down and accept them as if these have come down to you from heaven."[11]

Usman's reflections on history writing began with a critique of the late-nineteenth-century German scholar-explorer Heinrich Barth. Usman was aware that virtually every major Western scholar writing on Africa in the 1950s and 1960s considered Barth a virtually unimpeachable source. Robert Rotberg said Barth was "steeped . . . in the history of the people he traveled among." Philip Curtin praised Barth's scholarship for the contemporary way in which "he makes use of ethnographic, linguistic and documentary evidence to solve problems of African history." Anthony Kirk-Greene lauded Barth's "empathy with Africans and Africa as his outstanding quality and a model for Europeans living in Africa today." Above all, Thomas Hodgkin heralded Barth as "Nigeria's greatest historian who—so far as northern Nigeria is concerned—constructed the frame of reference within which all later historical work has been done."[12]

To show why it was important to acknowledge the historicity of concepts used by historians, particularly those in the postcolonial period, Usman focused on Heinrich Barth's "great pre-occupation with . . . physical and genetic characteristics."

Barth had begun with the assumption "that the members of the ruling class would belong to a race distinct from the 'subject population'" and concluded that this difference "should be manifest in their physical characteristics and general bearing and conduct." But when "many of the members of the ruling class [he] met did not fit into the arch-type [he] had assumed," Barth's response was to "explain this discrepancy between his assumptions and what he found, in terms of miscegenation." This explanation, Usman argued, arose not from the nature of history in precolonial Sudanic Africa but from the racist biases undergirding dominant traditions in nineteenth-century European history writing. These biases explained the assumptions driving "writings on society and history in Sudan," that the "basic units of the society and history are races, nations, and tribes." Indeed, "in Barth's conception, major historical changes are rooted in changes in relations of conflict and warfare, subjugation and absorption between races and tribes."[13]

The preoccupation with race and tribe was part of a larger preoccupation, one with tradition. "The dominant perception of Nigerian history," argued Usman, "is that before colonial conquest the peoples in this country lived in what are called 'traditional societies.' These 'traditional societies' are all seen to be made up of tribes or ethnic groups of various sizes and degrees of relationship with each other."[14] When employed in historical writing, tradition served one of two purposes. The first was to justify the prejudice that African society was stagnant and that all change was driven from above. Historians contrasted an unchanging community with a dynamic state as the real site of changes. Second, appeal to an unchanging tradition was part of a presumption that this dynamic state was inevitably a product of external influences. Tradition also served as a rhetorical device: since every piece of historical writing had to begin at some point, the background to this point ceased to have historical movement, but became "tradition." Usman argued that the discourse on tradition was actually an admission of historical ignorance. In his doctoral thesis, Usman narrated the political history of Katsina, starting with autonomous towns in the fourteenth century. "Composed of distinct lineages and occupational groups," the authority of autonomous towns was "associated with particular religious cults." This system "was transformed in about mid-15th century" to the Sarauta System (1450–1804 AD) where the "various *Sarautu* (public offices) centered around the office of the Sarkin Katsina (King, or Lord of Katsina)." The office holders under the Sarauta System "were largely made up . . . of slaves and free men," and the government was run largely by "a bureaucracy of slaves, eunuchs and free-born commoners." The Sarauta System was overthrown by a movement that developed from 1796 to 1804 and was "led largely by intellectuals, the *mallamai*, under the leadership of Shehu Usman Danfodio." Known as the Jama'a, this movement was later ethnicized by its opponents who came to call it "the Fulani." Finally, with the growth of an aristocratic element, there developed the Emirate

System (c. 1816–1903) with the Emir of Katsina, a lieutenant of the caliph at Sokoto. After periodizing the post-fourteenth-century history of Katsina into five distinct epochs, Usman pointed out the problem of a tradition-driven narrative: "If you want to say what is the traditional political system in Katsina, for example, you will have to identify which of the five to choose."[15]

All talk of tradition simply ossifies systems as "fixed and unchanging" when they are always in historical flux. Even more, these systems are "racialized and tribalized" for "people don't only talk of the Katsina, Benin or the Oyo [traditional] political systems, or the political system of the various Tars of the Tiv, they talk in terms of the Hausa or the Yoruba or Edo political systems. . . . The institution of the Oba, the institution of the Sarki, is made [a] peculiar institution(s) of the Yoruba and the Hausa. And once you get into this attitude of making political systems, things, which are historically defined, as peculiar to a particular people, you end up by talking of the particular genius of particular peoples and you end up with racism. . . . While one admits that people who speak a common language share similarities at the level of concepts, there are similarities in some ideas; but when you are talking about political, economic and social organizations we have to be on a much firmer ground."[16]

But the talk of tradition was not just an ossification and a mis-signaling of the past. More than a way of sanctifying a particular past, the talk of tradition was about justifying a particular present: "What is believed to be traditional society is not something that has existed in any past. It is essentially what has existed in the colonial and neo-colonial present."[17] Usman went on to argue that the contemporary significance of tradition was political; it was part of an overall effort to check the integrative effects of a market economy: "the policy they adopted toward settlement reveal clearly that the British were working to block the process of integration which had already been taking place and which had been affected by the introduction of the colonial economy." Market formation and the process of integration had been the subject of a dissertation by another ABU historian, Mahmud Tukur, who pointed out that both processes had long preceded colonial rule: "Zaria had communities of Nupe and Yoruba speaking people in Birnin Zaria itself, people who had been there for several centuries, and some of whom had become Zazzagawa of Nupe and of Yoruba origin, but Zazzagawa all the same." With the building of the railway in the colonial period, there was an increased inflow of immigrants into Zaria "from all parts of Nigeria." This is how the Sabon Gari developed, though "we are not sure what it was called at that time." The British sought to check this process administratively: first they decreed "that people who were not indigenes of the area could not live in Zaria City itself." They followed with another regulation in the 1920s to the effect that "Muslims must not live in Sabon Gari" but move to Tudun Wada.[18]

Usman sought to historicize the discussion on political

identities. In a critique of M. G. Smith, Usman pointed out that "the dominant categories used in the writings on the societies and history of Central Sudan are 'Hausa,' 'Fulani,' 'Habe,' 'Kanuri,' 'Tuareg' and others of this type." A one-dimensional view that sees the historical process exclusively through ethnic and racial categories blunts its full diversity. So long as these societies are seen as "amalgams of ethnic groups in relations of domination or subordination to one another," it is "not possible to grapple with the historical process of the genesis and movement of the political communities of the central Sudan." The historian is reduced to a gatherer of data, which is predetermined by and in turn reinforces "the assumption that the basic movement of African history and societies is the struggle and conflict of ethnic groups."[19] If you take identities existing in the present period as a given, then generalize them across historical time, how would it then be possible to understand the process of identity formation over time and relate it to the larger process of cultural change, economic development, and political transformation?

If it could be shown that people lived in multi-ethnic communities, what would be the reason to hold on to the prejudice that kinship was the only key to understanding their lives—social, political, and cultural? "If History is about the economic, political and cultural activity of people how could people living together and taking part in the same activities not share a common history or historical association?" he asked in his review of M. G. Smith's work. "If, however, M. G. Smith means by 'history' or 'historical association' the way historical activity or process is experienced and conceived he has to show why the settled Fulani would have a common experience with the nomadic Fulani; and the Mohameddan Habe with the pagan Habe, irrespective of their occupation, beliefs and location."[20]

Usman's writing offered an alternative way of understanding the historical movement of political communities in precolonial Africa. To make the point, he deconstructed key ethnic and racial categories, beginning with the Hausa-speaking Habe and the Fulfulde-speaking Fulani. "When we turn to genealogical origin, the Hausa-speaking people, the Habe, have no tradition of originating from a common ancestor."[21] The tradition they do have, at least from the seventeenth century, is one of speaking a common language. ". . . it is not clear when the name 'Hausa' began to be applied to the language now known as Hausa. Or, to which dialects of the language it was first applied. If we go by current usage in the western Hausa dialects, the name was probably first applied to these western dialects, or, to others which may have now disappeared. It is likely, however, that by the seventeenth century the notion of Hausa Bakwai had developed and the Kanawa would have been seen as belonging to this larger entity."[22] That, however, could not offer a sufficient clue to their political history. For a clue, one would need to look beyond language to locality. With "some of the Muslim and non-Muslim 'Habe' of Zazzau," the common origin was clearly "territorial or political but not genealogical."[23] Even with the Fulani, the role of genealogical origin as "a palpable factor in determining social solidarity" was limited to the level of the lineages and clans. In fact, Usman pointed out, the political history of the people called Fulani had been a key concern of scholars long before the colonial period: "Clearly the convergence of various elements like genealogical origin, territorial origin and language in the formation of the Fulfulde-speaking peoples was considered problematic among the Sakkwato scholars. It is from such issues that our examination must start."[24]

Neither the Habe nor the Fulani could be assumed to exist as cohesive language-based groups with no significant internal differences. Just as there were important differences between Muslim and non-Muslim Habe, so there were important differences shaping the histories of settled and nomadic Fulani. These differences, in turn, did not derive from genealogy but from locality. "A large proportion of the Fulfulde-speaking clans of the Kasar Hausa derived their identity not from any common genealogical origin but from the territory or town where they emerged as a distinct entity or with which they came to be closely associated."[25]

Usman claimed that the identity Fulani had changed over time, from a linguistic one in the eighteenth century to one identifying a political estate or an occupational group in the nineteenth century. The meaning of Habe, too, had to be looked for in changing historical developments: could it be that Habe had become more of a residual category, one enveloping all those not defined by the linguistic, cultural, or occupational category Fulani?[26] If so, then the historical evolution of Fulani and Habe as relational identities would have great resemblance with the historical evolution of Tutsi and Hutu in Central Africa, one an identity signifying the crystallization of privilege and the other its absence. The scholarly challenge was to locate the development of political identities in a historical understanding of the process of state formation. "We shall begin to face up to one of our important tasks; the creation of a conceptual framework with which the specific nature of the African historical and contemporary reality can be understood. Only with such an understanding can the people of this continent forge political communities suited to their needs and situation in the present epoch."[27]

The task had already been taken on board by two pioneering scholars: Kenneth Onwuka Dike at the University of Ibadan and Abdullahi Smith, the founder of the Department of History at Ahmadu Bello University in Zaria. Dike published his 1950 doctoral thesis as a book in 1956, *Trade and Politics in the Niger Delta, 1830–1885: An Introduction to the Economic and Political History of Nigeria*. Focusing on migration into the Niger Delta, Dike explained it as a consequence of land hunger on the one hand and slavery and the slave trade on the other. He showed how it led to the emergence of communities that transcended the old ethnic entities and how these polities could not be regarded as tribal. "Moreover, city-state is a more appropriate designation than 'tribal state,' since the period of migration

disorganized tribal entities and the slave trade further accentu-
ated the mingling of peoples. In the nineteenth century therefore, the Delta states were grouped not by contiguity and in the
period under survey citizenship came increasingly to depend
not on descent, but on residence."[28] If Igbo was not the designation of kinship but a category "which many of the constituent
groups have only recently and often reluctantly accepted as
their ethnic identity,"[29] if there was a problem in using "single
entities as Igbo religion or political system,"[30] as Dike pointed
out and, if, as Usman reflected on Dike's thesis, these various
groups have become ethnically Igbo during the past eighty
years, then all these observations led to the same conclusion:
the problem of using Igbo as an ethnographic entity.

Colonial preoccupation with "restoration and rehabilitation
of cultural heritage" tends to reify culture, robbing it of historical dynamism. It "actually perpetuates the ethos of dependence which it is ostensibly intended to eliminate." Usman
claimed that such an approach was marked by "three basic
weaknesses," which he listed as follows: "its ahistoricity; its
transcendental definition of culture which makes culture
peripheral and marginal; and its racialization and tribalization
of culture. . . . When it is closely examined, it would be realized that it involves a denial of history and historical movement because culture is perceived as a given dimension of a
people's existence and not a product of historical existence and
development with specificity for each epoch."[31]

The tradition of designating African political communities

as tribal went alongside a widespread consensus among colonial scholars that Africans lacked the capacity for political association beyond kin groups, and that all evidence of stable political communities in the past had to be ascribed to statemaking by racially distinct group of outsiders, called Hamites. Under this explanation could be grouped all kinds of local historiographies, from those of Berber migrations in West Africa to those of Arabization in Sudan to the Tutsi migration in Central Africa. As late as 1963, the supposed deans of African history, Roland Oliver and John D. Fage, had written a book titled *A Short History of Africa*, in which they summed up the basic thesis that has come to be known as the "Hamitic Hypothesis," and from which Usman quoted in detail:

> Stretching right across sub-Sahara Africa from the Red Sea to the mouth of the Senegal, and right down to the central highland spine of Bantu Africa from the Nile sources to southern Rhodesia, we find the axis of what we call the Sudanic civilization . . . the incorporation of the various African peoples concerned into states whose institutions were so similar that they must have derived from a common source. . . . In a very real sense, therefore, the "sudanic" state was a superstructure erected over village communities of peasant cultivators rather than a society which had grown up naturally out of them. In many cases such states are known to have had their origin in conquest; in almost

all other cases conquest must be suspected. . . . Its earliest propagators seemed to have moved southwards from the Nile Valley. . . .[32]

Abdullahi Smith had written of how colonial historiography had "accepted uncritically the simple hypothesis that that this history is merely the story of the way in which a group of Hamitic (Berber) invaders from the Sahara imposed a state-like structure on a number of politically segmented Negro peoples in the Central Sudan."[33] Abdullahi Smith went on to mock this convention: "Much prominence is given to the stories of the foreign hero who comes from afar (as the British did more recently) and with his magic sword or his mandate from the god of the sky or his supernatural power otherwise derived, imposes himself and his progeny on a previously unorganized people creating new allegiances among them and mustering them into new communities in the form of states."[34] This is how Usman summed up the impact of this scholarship: "It seems that what you had existing in most parts of Nigeria were not groups which were essentially defined in kinship terms but groups whose fundamental identity was tied up with their mode of existence. Increasingly it is becoming clear to us that territoriality and occupation played a central role. And anybody who has looked at Nigerian history knows that kinship played a powerful role at the level of ideology."[35]

Postcolonial Nigerian historiography has provided us with the outlines of an alternative to the theory of kinship identified with the anthropological school that built on the work of Henry Maine. As I have tried to show, it accomplished this through the efforts of three seminal thinkers: Kenneth Dike, Abdullahi Smith, and, above all, Yusuf Bala Usman.[36] In my view, the approach they pioneered is based around three statements.

First, kinship as a basis of association was never strictly descent-based, even in the ancient era. As Maine himself noted, even in Rome, *patria potestas* was never just a blood category; it included slaves and those adopted into the family. But when it came to the colonies, Maine insisted on the purity of phenomena; thus his insistence on privileging evidence from the isolated but uncontaminated interior over that from the cosmopolitan and therefore contaminated coast of India. Similarly with Heinrich Barth writing on Katsina: as Usman remarked, Barth expected the rulers to be of a race different from subjects, and when he found that they were not, he blamed it on miscegenation. These intellectuals had constructed a binary between the West and the non-West, one based less on observation than on conception, so much so that the same observations were interpreted in sharply opposite ways: developments ascribed to urbanization, cosmopolitanism, and progress in the West were seen as outcomes of impurity and miscegenation in the non-West. As Nigerian historiography showed, the alternative was to see kinship as porous and historical, rather than as closed and unchanging.

Second, this scholarship pointed out that even where it

existed as a form of political association, kinship was never universal, whether in the West or the non-West. All three Nigerian scholars we have referenced were at pains to outline the existence of multiple paths to the formation of political communities in West Africa: if political identities in some cases were kin-based, in other cases they were place-based. "In Lagos state," wrote Usman, "you would find Nigerians who were Lagosians by identity and who spoke Yoruba, but who may not be Yoruba by origin. Similarly, you would find in Kano State Nigerian citizens who were 'Kanawa' (people of Kano) and spoke Hausa, but who may actually be Igbo, Yoruba, or, some other ethnic origin."[37] In his 2000 book, *The Misrepresentation of Nigeria*, Usman critiqued fundamental dichotomies that represented the competition and conflict between North and South, ethnic nationalities, and Christians and Muslims as inevitable: ". . . before the coming into being of Nigeria, there was no ethnic nationality called 'Hausa,' as was the case today. Instead, what we had were Kanawa, people of Kano; Katsinawa, people of Katsina; Zage-Zagi, people of Zazzau; Sakkatawa, people of Sokoto, etc. The same really applied to the Yoruba, who were identified as Egba, Oyo, Ekiti, Ijebu, etc." All available records indicated that the word "Yoruba" (originally, "Yarriba") was a Hausa language name for the people of the Alafinate of Oyo, first used by a seventeenth-century Katsina scholar, Dan Masani.[38] Indeed, Bala maintained that contemporary ethnic nationalities were actually created in the process of the formation of the colonial state in Nigeria.

The third and overarching statement of this school was to read diversity not as evidence of deviation (and therefore an impurity in a sea of purity) but of a different historical route, thereby recognizing the existence of multiple routes and plural histories.

NATIONALISM AND STATECRAFT

Indirect rule had been an overarching and ambitious mode of rule. I have argued that its theory was anchored in a racialized and tribalized historiography, and its governance was based on an administrative practice that divided African colonies into tribal homelands and the population of each homeland into native and non-native tribes. The customary regime discriminated in favor of native tribes and against non-natives systematically. This is why the formulation of an alternative historiography would not be enough to overcome the colonial political legacy; it also required an alternative political practice, one that would create a form of citizenship adequate to building an inclusive political community.

The debate on postcolonial citizenship took place primarily in oppositional movements faced with the urgency of building political support through internal organization or external alliances. Following the massacre of nearly two hundred thousand Hutu students in Burundi in 1972, the Kinyarwanda-speaking minority in Congo ceased to identify itself through a cultural discourse on origin, as Banyarwanda (those from

Rwanda), and began to identify itself territorially, in the present and politically, as Banyamulenge (those who live in Mulenge). In Uganda, during the guerrilla war led by the National Resistance Army from 1981 to 1986 and thereafter, a similar shift occurred in the identification of rural populations, from one based on dissent and origin to residence, in response to questions such as "Who can vote?" "Who can run for office?"[39] In Nigeria, when those active against the military demanded that a Sovereign National Conference (SNC) be called to discuss constitutional issues, the debate focused on the constituent elements—the building blocks—of Nigerian society that should be represented at the SNC.[40]

One country, mainland Tanzania, led by Mwalimu Julius Nyerere, successfully implemented an alternative form of statecraft. I consider it the most successful attempt to dismantle the structures of indirect rule through sustained but peaceful reform. In an era when it was fashionable to think of violence as the way to "smash the colonial state," Nyerere taught otherwise: first, that the backbone of the colonial state and its legacy was not the army and the police but its legal and administrative apparatus, and that it required political vision and political organization—not violence—to "smash" these. The creation of a substantive law from multiple sources— precolonial life, colonial modern form of the state, and anticolonial resistance—and the establishment of a single and unified law-enforcing machinery meant that every citizen in mainland Tanzania was governed on the basis of the same set of rules, enforced by a single court system. Here, I intend to focus on Nyerere's seminal achievement: creating an inclusive citizenship and building a nation-state.

Assessments of Julius Nyerere, Tanzania's first president, are conventionally focused on his quest for *ujamaa*, a just social order based on community solidarity. Whereas supporters hailed *ujamaa* as a creative adjustment of socialist thought to local realities, critics contemptuously dismissed it as a romantic and unscientific endeavor. Nyerere himself once quipped that "If Marx were born in Tanzania he would have written the Arusha Declaration." I will argue that Nyerere's concern with social justice needs to be understood in the context of his overriding commitment to building a nation-state. Nyerere was, above all, a statesman, more the father of the nation-state *(baba wa taifa)* as ordinary people understood him than the prophet of a new social order, which is how his intellectual supporters and critics often cast him. In his farewell address to the Tanzanian parliament on July 29, 1985, Julius Nyerere—affectionately called *Mwalimu* (teacher) by his people—recalled his ambition at Tanzania's independence: "the single most important task which I set out in my Inaugural Address in December 1962 was that of building a united nation on the basis of human equality and dignity."[41]

By "equality and dignity," Mwalimu understood, above all, equality in the face of law, or, put differently, equality in spite of differences and privileges—those based on race and tribe—institutionalized and enforced by colonial law. Nyerere's political career can be divided into several stages. I will focus on two of these. The key issue in the opening stage was the political status of *race*. Faced with widespread and popular demands for race-based affirmative action, Nyerere insisted on doing away with all race-based distinctions in civil law. It brought Nyerere face to face with the most serious political crisis of his life, triggered by the 1964 army mutiny that drew significant support from the organized workers' movement. Pivotal to the second phase was the political status of *tribe*. To do away with ethnic-based distinctions in customary law, Nyerere mounted a political project that did away with native authorities. The objective was to build a centralized state structure, one that would do away with the colonial legacy of a division between customary and civil law on the one hand and civil and native authorities on the other. The state-building project, as we shall see, was at the expense of democracy and social justice *(ujamaa)*, both of which featured highly in Nyerere's public speeches. Nyerere was, above all, a militant nationalist determined to build a centralized territorial state and a common citizenship in the face of a colonial legacy defined by politically and legally enforced racial and tribal privilege.

The political status of race became a key issue in the period leading to independence. It distinguished the main nationalist party, the Tanganyika African National Union (TANU), from challenges to its right and left. To the right was the United Tanganyika Party (UTP), which embraced the colonial vision of a racialized political order, dressed up as multiracialism, whereby political rights flowed first and foremost from one's officially defined racial identity. To the left was the populist African National Congress (ANC), which championed a nativist political agenda whereby citizenship in the independent state would be confined to the majority native population, *Africans*. From the racialized colonial definition of African would follow the answer to the question: Who is a Tanganyikan?

Three key events defined the struggle between these political tendencies. The first was TANU's decision to participate in the racially based election of 1958. The second was the 1961 parliamentary debate over how to define citizenship, whether in terms of race or residence. The third was the 1961–1964 struggle for affirmative action in favor of the native majority, a program called Africanization. The cumulative outcome was the army mutiny of 1964.

It is worth remembering that the political party that led Tanganyika's independence struggle, TANU, excluded Asian and European residents of the country from membership right up to independence. Though TANU's membership policy was altered in 1956 to admit persons of mixed African and another race, the door remained closed on persons of Asian and European origin. Individuals of Asian origin may have been prominent in the independence struggle,[42] but they were barred from membership in TANU. On its part, the colonial state championed a policy that promised equal treatment between races, but not between individuals. This policy was known as "multi-racialism" and was justified as a guarantee of parity between races.[43] In his denunciation of the UTP, Nyerere argued that racial parity would "entrench and perpetuate racialism" rather than create a "democratic partnership which recognizes the basic rights of the individual regardless of his or her colour or creed."[44] From this point of view, participation in the multiracial 1958–1959 election was a strategic compromise, presumably made because it afforded Nyerere the chance to support like-minded Asian and European politicians and at the same time oppose the growing challenge from the ANC to the left. The leadership of the ANC called for citizenship to be restricted to the indigenous population and, as a consequence, a state racially defined by an all-African government and an all-African civil service, and a society restructured through a redistribution of wealth and income from the historically privileged non-native (European and Asian) minorities to the historically oppressed and disadvantaged native (African) majority. Demanding "Africa for the Africans," its press release of August 12, 1960, declared: "Our people have suffered exploitation from colonial imperialists for over forty years and even today are still economically enslaved by the Asians."[45] Avowing a more moderate position on the race question, TANU withdrew its support from *Mwafrika*, the main ANC-linked Swahili newspaper supporting the independence struggle, and founded a new paper, *Ngurumo*, in 1959.[46] In the eyes of the colonial state, the consequence of this was to establish TANU as a moderate alternative to the extremist ANC. Speaking on the radio on his inauguration as Tanganyika's first elected chief minister, Nyerere assured

Asians and Europeans: "Militant nationalism has been combined with a smile and good humour. . . . The people of Tangayika became fervent nationalists without becoming racialists."[47] His cabinet included a European and an Asian, even though neither was allowed to join TANU.

The National Assembly debate over how to define citizenship took place in October 1961, two months before independence. The question before parliament was clear: should citizenship be based on race or residence? The ANC stood for the former; Nyerere and his supporters for the latter. During the debate, the ANC called for priority for "indigenous inhabitants" over "other races who have made their homes in Tanganyika." Individual members (such as Christopher Tumbo) demanded that immigrant races be required to register and naturalize themselves with the Council of Chiefs which had the right to accept or reject their applications. Others questioned whether Asian citizens would be willing to "shoot the Indians in India for the sake of Tanganyikans," and that "the common man" saw Asians as having divided loyalties, with "one leg in Tanganyika and one leg in Bombay." Nyerere is said to have lost his temper, most uncharacteristically, and denounced his opponents sharply: "If we are going to base citizenship on colour we will commit a crime. Discrimination against human beings because of their colour is exactly what we have been fighting against. . . . They are preaching discrimination as a religion to us. And they stand like Hitlers and begin to glorify the race. We glorify human beings, not colour." He then threatened to resign if the proposed law was rejected. [48]

In 1959, there were 299 civil service administrative officers in the highest ranks of the civil service in Tanganyika; of these, only seven were black Tanganyikans. The Africanization debate in parliament unfolded against this background. The terms of the debate were set in 1962 when a European member of parliament, Bryceson, gave a speech in parliament arguing that Africanization meant the employment of local people, regardless of race. Both the ANC opposition and leaders of the Tanganyika Federation of Labour (TFL) denounced Bryceson and were joined by several TANU members who insisted that "Africanization means Africanization, it does not in any way suggest localization." The ANC press release stated unequivocally: "Africans cannot progress unless special privileges and protections are given to them so as to enable them to catch up with the progress of non-Africans. Advanced and backward people cannot be treated equally because to do so would mean the continuance of the already existing inequality between them. Unequals cannot be treated equally." Nyerere tried to stake a middle ground, stating that black Tanganyikans should have preference in *new* appointments and promotions on the grounds that the racial composition of the civil service should reflect the country's population.[49] Matters reached a point where the ANC linked Nyerere's opposition to rapid Africanization to his relationship to British and U.S. officials, characterizing Nyerere as "the chief imperialist stooge and neo-colonialist tool and chief agent-perpetual leader of multiracial TANU." When Nyerere visited the United States for a month in 1960, and then again in 1963 at the invitation of the State Department, the ANC leader Zuberi Mtemvu visited China and other socialist countries in early 1961. The ANC's arguments resonated with trade union leadership as with many of TANU's middle-rank leaders. As provincial party officials joined trade unionists to demand for rapid Africanization, Nyerere faced a rapidly widening split in the ranks of TANU. Faced with the prospect of a split in the party, he chose to resign as prime minister after only forty-four days in office, returning to the party to purge it of dissidents while handing over the reins of government to Rashidi Kawawa, former president of the Tanganyika Federation of Labour. Kawawa quickened the tempo of Africanization, instituting a commission to ensure Africanization of the entire civil service. By June 1962, 40 percent of expatriate civil servants had left the country.[50]

Concessions on Africanization went alongside repression of dissent: new laws in June 1962 limited the right to strike, prevented civil servants from joining unions, gave the TFL greater power over member unions, and legalized preventive detention.[51] Mwesiga Baregu wrote that "in 1962, the liquidation of the opposition in Tanzania began in earnest" as the government "unleashed an onslaught on competing political parties, independent labour and local participatory organizations in the rural areas."[52] As he reorganized the party, Nyerere transferred several of the party leaders who had opposed his citizenship and Africanization policies to government posts. But the race question was not so easy to go away: tied up with privilege in the colonial period, race was the cutting edge of the demand for social justice in the postcolonial period. There were clear signs of a revived opposition when Christopher Tumbo, the former trade union leader and leading proponent of rapid Africanization, resigned his position as High Commissioner to Great Britain and returned to Tanganyika in August 1962 to form the People's Democratic Party (PDP). Its founding members included several ANC activists and its charter advocated racial policies on citizenship and Africanization. Tumbo denounced the new republican constitution he claimed made the president a virtual dictator. In January 1963, party leaders met to discuss plans to merge with the ANC.

That same month, Nyerere assumed office as the first president of Tanganyika. At the TANU Annual Delegates conference, Nyerere announced plans to introduce a one-party system and open up membership in TANU to all races. The ANC and the All-Muslim National Union of Tanganyika (AMNUT) demanded a referendum.[53] The government invoked the Preventive Detention Act to arrest key opposition leaders. Matters reached a head in January 1964 as Nyerere denounced Africanization as "a form of racial discrimination." In a letter to government ministries, he proclaimed: "the nation must use the entire reservoir of skill and experience. . . . The skin in which skill is encased is completely irrelevant. . . . This means that discrimination in civil service employment as regards recruitment, training and promotion must be brought to an end immediately. . . . We cannot allow the growth of first and second class citizenship. Africanization is dead."[54] The abortive military coup of January 20, 1964 followed less than two weeks later.

The crisis that followed was the most serious of Nyerere's political career. The trade union leadership responded swiftly. The railway union promised to resist the change "at all costs"; the local government union accused Nyerere of taking the country "back to the colonial days." There followed the mutiny led by the eight-hundred-man First Battalion. On the fifth day there were rumors that the trade unions were planning a general strike in alliance with the mutineers. Convinced that the government was in danger, Nyerere reversed an earlier decision and called for British military intervention. Within twelve hours, a force of less than sixty British marines began its assault on Colito Barracks. Ninety minutes later the mutiny had been crushed. The women were among the first to oppose the mutiny. For educated women, especially for those of European and Asian descent, the civil service offered one of the few opportunities for employment. The ANC had publicly opposed the practice of "married women being employed in both government and commercial offices, when there are many African men roaming in the town streets without employment."[55] Women of all races followed the leader of the national women's association, Bibi Titi Mohamed, and marched to the State House to show their whole-hearted "loyalty, devotion and allegiance" to Mwalimu Nyerere.

Once the mutiny was aborted, the military was reorganized (and British officers replaced); fifty policemen were implicated in the mutiny, and over two hundred union leaders were arrested. Christopher Tumbo of the Railway Workers Union spent four years in prison, while Victor Mkello of the Plantation Workers Union was banished to a remote area. Within a month of the mutiny, the government had restructured the labor movement: the TFL was dissolved and the TANU-controlled union, National Union of Tanganyika Workers (NUTA), set up in its place. A presidential commission on the one-party state was instituted, and the one-party state became a reality with the constitution of 1965.[56]

Politically and ideologically, the 1961–1964 debate on Africanization revolved around two terms: rights and justice. The demand for equal rights was framed around the formal equality of all citizens, whereas the call for justice pointed to the substantive inequality among citizens. Nyerere rejected outright any group-based notion of rights, on the grounds that group rights were associated with colonial racial policies, and called for individual rights rather than rights of communities.[57] And yet, the demand for group rights did not have to be race-based. There were also other group-based inequalities such as tribe, gender, and class. The period from the institution of the single-party state in 1965 to the Arusha Declaration in 1967 presents us with two ironies. The first is that party leaders like

Nyerere who advocated a liberal vision of racial equality and a racially inclusive view of citizenship had taken to illiberal measures. Nyerere usually justified his move to a single-party state as a reform that made it possible for Tanzanian citizens to elect the leadership of the party they overwhelmingly supported. But this was disingenuous since the move to a one-party state had come at a time of rising opposition to TANU policies. At another time, in a lighter moment, Nyerere conceded a different possibility. Responding to a toast by President Carter during a state visit to the American capital in August 1977, Nyerere remarked, "I have recently been reading some very good books about President Washington and his time, and I have come to the conclusion that the problems of young countries can be very similar. . . . I suspect he might even be able to understand better my one-party system than your multi-party system."[58]

There was also irony in that, faced with liberal rights-based critiques of the one-party state, Nyerere turned to a discourse on justice—the Arusha Declaration—to defend himself. As his critics on the left[59] well understood at the time, the Arusha Declaration was not a call for class-based justice, but one for national justice; justice for all its citizens, regardless of class, race or tribe. Just in case some harbored illusions, Nyerere warned in material he prepared for party study groups: "the [Arusha] Declaration is first of all a reaffirmation of the fact that we are Tanzanians and wish to remain Tanzanians as we develop. . . . This is very important, for it means that we cannot adopt any political 'holy book' and try to implement its rulings—with or without revision."[60] For Nyerere, the Arusha Declaration was part of a state-building project: "the Arusha Declaration and our democratic single-party system, together with our national language, Kiswaahili, and a highly politicized and disciplined national army, transformed more than 126 different tribes into a cohesive and stable nation."[61] Whether the language of public discourse evoked liberal or socialist values, Nyerere's primary political project remained what he had proclaimed in his inaugural speech, of which he reminded his audience in his farewell speech. It was a project neither to realize democracy nor social justice, but to build a sovereign centralized nation-state.

The second phase of nation-building in Tanzania opened with the Arusha Declaration and spanned the era of villagization. The very year of the Arusha Declaration, 1967, Nyerere wrote another political proclamation, a pamphlet titled *Socialism and Rural Development*, in which he called upon peasants to form *ujamaa* villages and to increase their productivity and welfare through collective self-help. "The essential thing is that the community would be farming as a group and living as a group," he wrote. The villagization project was initially cast in ideological terms—as a call for "collective self-help." But the response was poor: rich peasants found a way to turn the project to their advantage. The state responded to the lack of peasant enthusiasm with force. In turn, forced villagization provided the overall context in which state centralization proceeded, now at the local level.

It was clear in the very first year of villagization that little work had been done to prepare the ground for its implementation. A commentator in *The Drum* astutely observed: "What was to become of well-established farmers' fields and property? And how, in the first place, could rich farmers be persuaded to join a fledging communal village? How would an *ujamaa* village's income be divided? How would slovenly workers be punished? How was private work to be treated?" Only one-hundred-and-eighty *ujamaa* villages had been established by the end of 1968. Most were small—with between thirty and forty families. Participation was limited to those with a highly politicized commitment to communal work. After the first flush of political excitement, the ground shifted, making for a very different kind of communal village. Often started by rich peasants, "these villages had only a minimal commitment to communal work and were started in order to get service such as running water, schools, clinics, and other large capital investments promised to villages by the government." When this, too, had run its course, the government took to compulsion. This created a third kind of village.[62]

The resort to compulsion developed in the course of disaster relief when officials declared that peasants whose old settlements had been destroyed by natural catastrophes would receive relief only *after* they had moved into new villages. In September 1973 the TANU Biennial Conference resolved that by the end of 1976 the whole rural population should live in villages.[63] The results were telling. The number of Tanzanians living in villages in 1970 was just over half a million, less than 5 percent of the mainland population. By 1974, the number had gone up to about two million, or 14 percent of the total population. In the year after the compulsory regime began in 1973, the number of villagers stood at about nine million, or 60 percent of the population. In 1977, those living in villages represented an estimated 79 percent of the mainland population. But compulsion had a catastrophic economic consequence. A single figure testified to this: in 1970, Tanzania *exported* 540,000 tons of surplus maize. By 1974 the country was forced to *import* 400,000 tons of food grains, including 300,000 tons of maize. Between 1970 and 1975, total per capita food production fell to its 1960 level.[64]

That villagization proceeded in the face of this adversity is testimony that its real returns were political, not economic. Villagization proceeded in tandem with the expansion of the state apparatus to localities. Ironically, this expansion and strengthening of the local state apparatus—undertaken in 1972 at the height of forced villagization—was called "decentralization" and was designed by McKinsey and Company, a leading American consultancy firm. In reality, it was an extreme centralization that extended the state apparatus to districts, did away with native authorities, and subordinated the party to the state apparatus.[65]

Forced villagization turned out to be integral to the

trajectory of nation-building in Tanzania. Whereas forced vil-lagization provided the rationale for the extension of central state institutions to rural areas, it was also testimony to the failure of the democratic project in the post-colonial period. Having failed to generate widespread consent for the socio-economic project called *ujamaa*, Nyerere and the state leader-ship resorted to top-down compulsion to stifle all opposition to villagization. To this extent then, we must qualify the claim that Nyerere provided a "peaceful" way to reform the colonial state. Nyerere's insight was to grasp that the heart of colonial governance was its legal and administrative, and not military, apparatus; if the legal and administrative apparatus was not reformed, the colonial state would continue to exist even if the colonial military, police and prison officials left Tanzania. I have argued that Nyerere's state-building project developed in two phases: the first focused on the political status of race, and the second on the political status of tribe. In both instances, Nyerere was not averse to using direct force when he failed to generate sufficient popular support to realize the state-building project. To that extent, the state-building project in the Tan-zania of Nyerere must be seen as the outcome of a mixed strategy of statecraft, based on consent as well as coercion.

When forced villagization wreaked havoc on the rural economy, the state turned to foreign donors, inviting each donor agency to "adopt" a region for "development."[66] Nyerere recalled the milestones of this process in his July 1985 farewell speech: "In 1972, after localization of staff had made some progress, we decentralized Central Government administration to Regional and District level, at the same time abolishing the old Local Government system. In 1975, through the Villagization Act, we laid the basis for Village Governments." And then added: "But by 1982 we realized that we had made a major error in abolishing Local Government; this Parliament therefore passed legislation to re-establish Local Government at District and Urban level, leaving the other systems basically intact."[67] Systems left intact were those that had replaced the colonial native authority.

The reform also created a single integrated legal structure. The colonial practice of merging administrative and judicial functions in the native authority was done away with as was the separation of civil and customary law.[68] A new substantive law was forged from a variety of sources: colonial law (civil and customary), precolonial customs, and the tradition of the anticolonial struggle. Nyerere took great pride in this development, telling parliament in his farewell speech: "this is a secular state.... The Bill of Rights which is incorporated in the new Constitution outlaws any racial or tribal or religious discrimination. We are now a nation of citizens absolutely equal before the law in theory and practice."[69]

As "father of the nation," Nyerere was seen to embody *raison d'état*. Part of this was the nation-state's claim to sovereignty, one that he was quick to assert in the face of superpower ambition and overreach. He lost no opportunity to call for the sovereign equality of states, especially in his dealings with Soviet and American officialdom. A member of the Russian Academy of Sciences recalled an encounter at the Soviet embassy in Dar es Salaam in the aftermath of the Soviet intervention of 1968: "He [Nyerere] went on to note that Tanzania believed firmly in strict observance of the UN Charter, in particular, its main principle: non-interference in the internal affairs of other states and respect for their sovereignty. He emphasized that this principle should be strictly observed by all states without exception, including great powers. He then recalled the principled position taken by Tanzania in connection with the American aggression in Vietnam."[70] A decade later, Nyerere was the first African head of state to visit Washington, D.C. after the election of Jimmy Carter as president. Responding to a toast by President Carter that August 1977, Nyerere tried to complement his host while airing long-standing concerns regarding big power ambitions: "If you don't mind me saying it: where the law of the jungle still reigns, the pygmies are very wary of the giants. . . . Your coming to the White House, Mr. President, has not changed the international law of the jungle, but our apprehensions have been greatly reduced by your coming to the White House."[71]

I have already said that Nyerere needs to be understood first and foremost as a state-builder and not a democrat or a social visionary. For the present generation, a single political fact should suffice to highlight Mwalimu Nyerere's seminal political achievement. This achievement is best understood against the backdrop of colonial legal and administrative practices. We have seen that the indirect rule state identified the population it governed as members of a group, either a race or a tribe. It ascribed rights and duties to groups, not to individuals. When it came to the political domain, punishments too were meted to groups, and not just individuals. Not surprisingly, where the legal and administrative order remained unchanged, these practices were only exacerbated by the introduction of representative political institutions at independence. In the face of growing political opposition, it became a convention to identify, brand and target the race or tribe of individual opponents. It created a regional political environment marked by ethnic cleansing and extreme violence. To this general tendency, there was one exception: mainland Tanzania. The political credit for this, I believe, goes to Mwalimu Nyerere. Whether or not Nyerere's achievement, the creation of a common political citizenship and a law-based order, turns out to be durable will depend on the capacity of subsequent generations to fashion a politics beyond the nation-state, one equal to realizing social justice. This, however, is a question that remains outside the scope of this small book.

Notes

Introduction

1. "Introduction," to W. E. B. Du Bois, *The World and Africa*, The Oxford W. E. B. Du Bois Series, Henry Louis Gates, Jr., ed. (New York: Oxford University Press, 2007).

2. Mahmood Mamdani, *When Does a Settler Become a Native? Reflections on the Colonial Roots of Citizenship in Equatorial and South Africa* (Inaugural Lecture, May 13, 1998, University of Cape Town, New Series No. 208).

ONE *Nativism: The Theory*

1. Irfan Habib, "The Coming of 1857," *Social Scientist*, vol. 26, no. 1 (Jan.-April, 1998) 6; cited in William Dalrymple, *The Last Mughal* (London: Bloomsbury, 2006), 10.

2. Henry Sumner Maine, "India," in Humphrey Ward, ed., *The Reign of Queen Victoria: A Survey of Fifty Years of Progress*, 474, 478; also cited in Karuna Mantena, *Alibis of Empire: Henry Maine and the Ends of Liberal Imperialism* (Princeton: Princeton University Press, 2010), 50.

3. Maine, "The Effects of Observation of India on Modern European Thought," in Maine, *Village Communities in the East and West, with Other Lectures, Addresses and Essays*, 3rd ed. (London: John Murray), 216–217.

4. Ibid., 211.

5. Ibid., 211, 216, 217, 218.

6. Ibid., 220, 224.

7. Ibid., 214.

8. Ibid., 215, 216.

9. Ibid., 215.

10. Ibid., 210.

11. Maine, *Village Communities in the East and West*, 56–57.

12. Dante J. Scala, "Introduction" to Henry Sumner Maine, *Ancient Law* (first published 1866, New Brunswick and London: Transaction Publishers, 2004), viii; see Mantena, *Alibis of Empire*, 14.

13. Christopher A. Bayly, "Maine and Change in Nineteenth-Century India," in Alan Diamond, ed., *The Victorian Achievement of Sir Henry Maine: A Centennial Reappraisal* (Cambridge: Cambridge University Press, 1991), 393. See discussion of "culture talk" in Mahmood Mamdani, *Good Muslim, Bad Muslim: America, the Cold War and the Roots of Terror* (New York: Pantheon, 2004), chap. 1.

14. Maine, *Village Communities in the East and West*, 9.

15. Maine, *Ancient Law* (first published 1866, New Brunswick and London: Transaction Publishers, 2004), 3, 9, 13, 14, 21.

16. "There is some evidence that the races which were subsequently united under the Persian monarchy, and those which peopled the peninsula of India, had all their heroic age and their era of aristocracies; but a military and a religious oligarchy appear to have grown up separately, nor was the authority of the king generally superseded. Contrary, too, to the course of events in the West, the religious element in the East tended to get the better of the military and the political." Maine, *Ancient Law*, 11.

17. "The Hindoo code, called the Laws of Manu, which is certainly a Brahmin compilation, undoubtedly enshrines many genuine observances of the Hindoo race, but the opinion of the best contemporary Orientalists is, that it does not, as a whole, represent a set of rules ever actually administered in Hindostan. It is, in great part, an ideal picture of that which, in the view of the Brahmins, *ought* to be the law." In contrast, "the Roman Code was merely an enunciation in words of the existing customs of the Roman people." Maine, *Ancient Law*, 17–18.

18. "Ethnology shows us that the Romans and the Hindoos sprang from the same original stock, and there is indeed a striking resemblance between what appear to have been their original customs. Even now, Hindoo jurisprudence has a substratum of forethought and sound judgment, but irrational imitation has engrafted in it an immense apparatus of cruel absurdities. From these corruptions the Romans were protected by their Code." Maine, *Ancient Law*, 20.

19. Maine, *Ancient Law*, 16–17.

20. Ibid., 77.

21. "We can see that Brahaminical India has not passed beyond a stage which occurs in the history of all the families of mankind, the stage at which a rule of law is not yet discriminated from a rule of religion. . . . In China this point has been passed, but progress seems to have been there arrested, because the civil laws are coextensive with all the ideas of which the race is capable." Then again: "Among the Hindoos, the religious element in law has acquired a complete dominance." Maine, *Ancient Law*, 23, 192.

22. Maine, *Ancient Law*, 24.

23. Ibid., 22.

24. Maine, *Lectures on the Early History of Institutions* (4th ed., 1885, Honolulu: University Press of the Pacific, 2002), 30–31.

25. Ibid., 64.

26. Ibid., 1.

27. Maine, *Ancient Law*, 129.

28. Maine, *Lectures on the Early History*, 68.

29. Maine, *Ancient Law*, 183. ". . . society in primitive times was not what it is assumed to be at present, a collection of *individuals*. In fact, and in the view of the men who composed it, it was *an aggregation of families*." Maine, *Ancient Law*, 126.

30. Maine, *Ancient Law*, 258.

31. Ibid., 130.

32. Ibid., 131.

33. Maine, *Lectures on the Early History*, 65.

34. He recounted one such "remarkable detail which connects the Irish with the Hindoo law" [and the Persian, too, as he went on to relate]: "This is the rule that a creditor who requires payment from a debtor of higher rank than himself shall 'fast upon him.' " In Persia, "a man intending to enforce payment of a demand by fasting begins by sowing some barley at his debtor's door and sitting down in the middle. The symbolism is plain enough. The creditor means that he will stay where he is without food, either until he is paid or until the barley-seed grows up and gives him bread to eat." The corresponding Indian practice is known as "sitting *dharna*": "The Brahmin who adopts this expedient for the purpose mentioned proceeds to the door or the house of the person against whom it is directed, or wherever he may most conveniently arrest him; he then sits down in dharna with poison or poignard or some other instrument of suicide in his hand, threatening to use it if his adversary should attempt to molest to pass him, he thus completely arrests him. In this situation the Brahmin fasts, and by rigor of the etiquette the unfortunate object of his arrest ought to fast also, and thus they both remain till the institutor of the dharna obtains satisfaction." Among the Irish, too, "the leading provision of the Senchus Mor" states: "Notice precedes every distress in the case of the inferior grades except it be by persons of distinction or upon persons of distinction. Fasting precedes distress in their case." Maine, *Lectures on the Early History*, 296–301.

35. Maine, *Lectures on the Early History*, 11.

36. Ibid., 226.

37. Ibid., 52–53.

38. Maine, *Ancient Law*, 170.

39. Thus it was that this indomitable intellect, who basked under the banner of cosmopolitanism and pluralism, could write: "Except the blind forces of nature, nothing moves in this world which is not Greek in origin." (Maine, "The Effects of Observation," *Village Communities*, 238).

40. *Ancient Law* included an extended discussion on three instruments—legal fiction, equity, and legislation—through which law combines the needs of stability with that of evolutionary change.

Legal fiction has made it possible for Roman law to combine semi-rigid sacredness with openness to change. At the same time, Maine argued that law requires a source of substantive values—equity—to infuse it with progressive tendencies and civilize it. This is what natural law gave to Roman law whereas the Greeks fell into the minutia of pure law, and the Hindoos lacked simplicity and symmetry.

41. Alfred C. Lyall, "Life and Speeches of Sir Henry Maine," *The Quarterly Review*, (April 1893), p. 290; cited in Mantena, *Alibis of Empire*, 166.

42. Maine, *Lectures on the Early History*, 359, 360.

43. Ibid., 361.

44. Ibid., 361.

45. Ibid., 362.

46. Ibid., 366–367.

47. Ibid., 367.

48. Ibid., 365.

49. Ibid., 380.

50. Ibid., 380–381.

51. Ibid., 382.

52. Ibid., 383.

53. Ibid., 392.

54. Ibid., 392.

55. Maine, "The Effects of Observation," *Village Communities*, 237.

56. "When, however, the rules which have to be obeyed once emanate from an authority external to the small natural group and forming no part of it, they wear a character wholly unlike that of a customary rule. They lose the assistance of superstition, probably that of opinion, certainly that of spontaneous impulse. The force at the back of law comes therefore to be a purely coercive force to a degree quite unknown in societies of the more primitive type. . . . As the conception of Force associated with order has been altered, so also, I think, has the conception of Order." Maine, *Lectures on the Early History*, 392–393.

57. Maine, *Lectures on the Early History*, 394.

58. Cyril H. Philips, Hira L. Singh, and Bishwa N. Pandey, eds., *The Evolution of India and Pakistan, 1858 to 1947: Select Documents* (1962), 11.

59. Between the last of the old rebellions in 1857 and first of the new nationalist agitations in 1906, the government of India altered its entire agrarian strategy, from the promotion of the free market to the protection of Indian institutions, regardless of their economic drawbacks. By the 1890s, the Revenue and Agriculture Department saw the village community, the subcaste, and the feudal estate as the only guarantee of India's social stability. Legislation protected the integrity of the village community by protecting the *biraderi*, the brotherhood, of cultivators against moneylenders (threatening to foreclose mortgages) and landlords (anxious to break down tenant rights). Tenancy acts set out rights of tenants, public registers of rights in land made it easy for them to defend these in court; cooperative societies provided alternative sources of credit; usury laws set limits to compound interest; and relief acts gave judges special powers to scale down their debts. The membership of each subcaste was defined; they were arranged in neat hierarchies; peasant castes were forbidden to sell land to commercial castes; martial castes were drawn into the army; disloyal castes were eased out of government jobs. The estate was protected by introducing primogeniture and by courts taking over encumbered estates to protect them from liquidation. Those desperate to maintain the cohesion of Indian society were followers of Sir Henry Maine. Sir Denzil Ibbetson, the moving force behind the Punjab Land Alienation Act, claimed that Maine's ideas about the evolution of property showed that the "fatal gift of individual property in land had been premature—and should be withdrawn, before the peasant proprietors of Punjab lost their land to trader-moneylenders." The hallmark achievement of this agrarian strategy was the passage of the Punjab Alienation of Land Act (1900), which prohibited land sales between members of different tribes (thus violating the most basic principle of laissez-faire and confirming caste formations). Septimus Smet Thorburn (1844–1924), the real architect of the

Punjab Alienation Act, sent copies of his book, *Mussalmans and Money-lenders in the Punjab* (1886), to every member of the Council of India. See Clive Dewey, "The Influence of Sir Henry Maine on Agrarian Policy in India," in Alan Diamond, ed., *The Victorian Achievement of Sir Henry Maine: A Centennial Reappraisal* (Cambridge: Cambridge University Press, 1991), 353–356, 370; also see John Lyons, "Linguistics and Law, the Legacy of Sir Henry Maine," in Diamond, ed., *The Victorian Achievement of Sir Henry Maine*, 303.

60. See Clive Dewey, "The Influence of Sir Henry Maine on Agrarian Policy in India," in Diamond, ed., *The Victorian Achievement of Sir Henry Maine*, 357.

61. Christopher A. Bayly, "Maine and Change in Nineteenth-Century India," See Dewey, "The Influence of Sir Henry Maine," in Diamond, ed., *The Victorian Achievement of Sir Henry Maine*, 396. William Dalrymple argues that Crown rule had begun by seeing the uprising as a Muslim conspiracy (440–443), proceeded to separate Hindu from Muslim and then to target the latter (420), first banning Muslims and then readmitting them to the city (460–463), in sum demonizing the Muslim (477–479). By the end of the nineteenth century, it had gone full circle to presenting itself as the protector of Muslims. William Dalrymple, *The Last Mughal* (London: Bloomsbury, 2006).

62. Sumit Sarkar, *Swadeshi Movement in Bengal*, 1903–1908; cited in Nick Dirks, "Colonial and Postcolonial Histories: Comparative Reflections on the Legacies of Empire," Global Background Report for the Human Development Report, 2004, *Building Inclusive Societies*, mimeo (Columbia University), 8.

63. Scott Alan Kugle, "Framed, Blamed and Renamed: The Recasting of Islamic Jurisprudence in Colonial South Asia, *Modern Asian Studies*, 35: 2 (May 2001), 257–313, 300–301.

64. Kugle, "Framed, Blamed and Renamed," 257–313, 263.

65. Dirks, "Colonial and Postcolonial Histories," 7.

66. Barbara D. Metcalf and Thomas R. Metcalf, *A Concise History of India* (Cambridge: Cambridge University Press, 2002), 158–159.

67. The argument is made in Nick Dirks, *Caste of Mind: Colonialism and the Making of Modern India* (Princeton: Princeton University Press, 2001).

68. Lilianne Fan, *Islam, Indigeneity, Legality, Native and Migrant Difference in the Making of Malay Identity* (Unpublished MA Thesis, Anthropology, Columbia University, 2004) 8, 15.

69. Michael B. Hooker, *The Personal laws of Malaysia* (1976), 62, cited in Fan, *Islam, Indigeneity, Legality*, 20.

70. Geoffrey Benjamin, "On Being Tribal in the Malay world," in Benjamin and Chou, eds., *Tribal Communities in the Malay World* (Leiden and Singapore, 2002), 44.

71. This paragraph and the next from Colin Nicholas in Benjamin and Chou, eds., *Tribal Communities in the Malay World* (Leiden and Singapore, 2002), 120.

72. "In the Malay world, the ability to claim exogenous origin therefore lends legitimacy to the right to rule. Sultans, nobles and prime ministers alike are not are not shy about their less-than-solely-Melayu origins. Contrariwise, to be fully indigenous *(asli)* implies that one is born to be ruled." Benjamin, "On Being Tribal," in Benjamin and Chou, eds., *Tribal Communities*, 20.

73. Fan, *Islam, Indigeneity, Legality*.

74. It had been preceded by an earlier resistance, the Java War in 1825, when Prince Diponegoro had risen in revolt against "infidel" colonial rule. The Dutch easily suppressed the so-called Java War; village unrest, however, fanned by Muslim scribes, continued to plague the colonial government in Java, the center of Dutch power. See J. M. van der Kroef, "Prince Diponegoro: Progenitor of Indonesian Nationalism," *Far Eastern Quarterly* (1949), 8: 430–433. Eduard S. de Klerck, *History of the Netherlands East Indies* (Rotterdam, 1938), 2: 342.

75. Christiaan Snouck Hurgronje, *The Achehnese*, A. W. S. Sullivan, trans. (Leiden: E. J. Brill, 1906), v.

76. Anna Lowenhaupt Tsing, "*Adat*/Indigenous," in Carol Gluck and Anna Lowenhaupt Tsing, eds., *Words in Motion: Towards a Global Lexicon* (Durham and London: Duke University Press, 2009), 41.

77. Snouck, *The Achehnese*, I: 10–11, 14, cited in Tsing, *"Adat/ Indigenous,"* in Gluck and Tsing, eds., *Words in Motion*, 50.

78. "The slowly but surely changing institutions of their society are thus revered as fixed and unchangeable by its individual units. But it is precisely in this connection that opportunity is given for continual disputes as to the *contents* of the *adat* [note: Cf. the remarks on the adat of the rulers of Mekka in my Mekka, vol. 1, p. 11 et seq.]. What is, in fact, the real and genuine *adat*, that which according to unimpeachable witnesses was formerly so esteemed, or that which the majority follow in practice at the present day, or that which many, by an interpretation opposed to that of the majority, hold to be lawful and permitted? Most questions of importance give rise to this three-fold query, and the answer is, as may be readily supposed, prompted by the personal interest of him who frames it." Christiaan Snouck Hurgronje, *The Achehnese*, A. W. S. Sullivan, trans. (Leiden: E. J. Brill, 1906), 1: 10.

79. Hurgronje, *The Achehnese*, 1: 16.

80. Ibid., 1: 94–95.

81. Ibid., 1: 153.

82. Hurgronje, *The Achehnese*, Part I, 1: 88.

83. Hurgronje, *The Achehnese*, 1: 159–160.

84. Hurgronje, *The Achehnese*, 2: 314.

85. Ibid., 2: 351.

86. Jaspen, cited in Eduard J. M. Schmutzer, *Dutch Colonial Policy and the Search for Identity in Indonesia* (Leiden: E. J. Brill, 1977), lii. (Fan, *Islam, Indigeneity, Legality, Native and Migrant Difference*, 2, 17, 11. 5).

87. Hurgronje, *The Achehnese*, 1: 166–167.

88. He pointed out the absence of a clerical establishment in Islam and the fact that officials in charge of administering Islamic worship and religious justice were traditionally the subordinates, rather than the superiors, of native rulers, and that neither they nor their masters were as a rule addicted to Muslim "fanaticism." Even the unattached *ulama*—like their counterparts in other Islamic lands—were independent and, as it were, otherworldly scribes and teachers, most of whom desired nothing better than to serve Allah in

peace. In other words, Indonesians, like other Muslims, did not owe sole allegiance to their religion. Everywhere and at all times the strict law of Islam had had to adapt itself to the traditional customs and mores, as well as to the political realities, governing the lives of its adherents. Thus while Koranic law had gained acceptance in the realm of marital and family law, in almost all other matters the Indonesian *adat* had prevailed. While there remained cause for fear, it would rightly be the fear of a small minority—especially of the fanatical *ulama*—dedicated to the notions of pan-Islam.

See "over panislamisme" (1910), 1: 364–380; see G. H. Bousquet and J. Schacht, eds., *Selected Works of C. Snouck Hurgronje* (Leiden, 1957). For a recent discussion, see Jans Prins, "Adat-law and Muslim Religious law in Modern Indonesia," *Welt des Islams*, N. S. (1951), 1: 283–300. A fuller treatment can be found in Hurgronje's larger work, *The Achehnese* (Leiden, 1906), 1: xvi. See, Harry J. Benda, "Christiaan Snouck Hurgronje and the Foundations of Dutch Islamic Policy in Indonesia," *The Journal of Modern History*, 30: 4 (December 1958), 338–347; also see by Benda, *The Crescent and the Rising Sun: Indonesian Islam Under the Japanese Occupation, 1942–45* (The Hague and Bandung, 1958), 32–99.

89. Tsing, "*Adat*/Indigenous," in Gluck and Tsing, eds., *Words in Motion*, 49.

90. Hurgronje, *The Achehnese*, 1: 14, cited in Tsing, "*Adat*/Indigenous," in Gluck and Tsing, eds., *Words in Motion*, 50.

91. Mona Abaza, "Ada/Custom in the Middle East and South Asia," in Tsing, "*Adat*/Indigenous," in Gluck and Tsing, eds., *Words in Motion*, 72.

92. Harko W. J. Sonius, "Introduction," in *Van Vollenhoven on Indonesian Adat Law*, ed., Johan F. Holleman (The Hague: Martinus Nijhoff, 1981), xxxvi, cited in Mona Abaza, "Ada/Custom in the Middle East and South Asia," in Tsing, "*Adat*/Indigenous," in Gluck and Tsing, eds., *Words in Motion*, 73.

93. Mona Abaza, "Ada/Custom in the Middle East and South Asia," in Tsing, "*Adat*/Indigenous," in Gluck and Tsing, eds., *Words in Motion*, 75.

TWO *Nativism: The Practice*

1. Karuna Mantena, *Alibis of Empire: Henry Maine and the Ends of Liberal Imperialism* (Princeton: Princeton University Press, 2010).

2. For a related argument, see, Ranajit Guha, *History at the Limits of World-History*, New York: Columbia University Press, 2003.

3. See David Laitin's study of "tradition" in Yorubaland. Laitin makes sense of the British choice of "traditional" allies in Yorubaland as the outcome of a policy that looked for those local elites most in danger of being sidelined. The point of allying with local elites that had legitimacy, but lacked authority, was to instrumentalize their legitimacy in return for reinforcing their weak authority. David Laitin, *Hegemony and Culture: Politics and Religious Change Among the Yoruba* (Chicago: Chicago University Press, 1986).

4. Eric Hobsbawm and Terence Ranger, *The Invention of Tradition* (Cambridge: Cambridge University Press, 1983).

5. Barthold Georg Niebuhr, *History of Rome*, 3 vols., (Philadelphia: Thomas Wardle, 1835).

6. "The history of political ideas begins, in fact, with the assumption that kinship in blood is the sole possible ground of community in political functions." Maine, *Ancient Law*, 129.

7. John Hannings Speke, *Journal of the Discovery of the Source of the Nile*, (New York: Harper and Brothers, Publishers, 1864), ix: 241–254.

8. See Tharcisse Gatwa, *The Churches and Ethnic Ideology in the Rwandan Crisis, 1900–1994* (PhD Dissertation, University of Edinburgh, 1998).

9. See Mahmood Mamdani, *When Victims Become Killers: Colonialism, Nativism and Genocide in Rwanda* (Princeton: Princeton University Press, 2001), 56.

10. Abdullahi Smith, "Some Considerations Relating to the Large-Scale Recording of Oral Traditions in the Northern States," in *A Little New Light* (Zaria: Abdullahi Smith Centre for Historical Research, 1987).

11. See Mamdani, *Saviors and Survivors: Darfur, Politics and the War on Terror* (New York: Pantheon, 2009).

12. Winston Churchill, *The River War: An Account of the Reconquest of the Sudan* (New York: Carroll and Graff Publishers, 2000).

13. Sir Harold A. MacMichael, *A History of the Arabs in the Sudan and Some Account of the People who Preceded Them and of the Tribes Inhabiting Darfur* (Cambridge, U.K.: The University Press, 1922, 2 vols.).

14. Ali Mazrui, *Euro-Jews and Afro-Arabs: The Great Semitic Divergence in World History* (Maryland: University Press of America, 2008).

15. In Sudanese state politics, the only serious attempt I know of to question the Arabization paradigm followed on the heels of the 1972 Addis Ababa agreement between the northern government and southern rebels. In a book presented to the OAU at its tenth anniversary, the ministry of foreign affairs of the Nimeiry government—under the leadership of Minister Mansour Khalid, and his deputies, Ali Abel and Francis Deng—consciously attempted to shift the paradigmatic focus of Sudanese history from assimilation, as in Arabization, to integration.

16. Sigmar Hillelson, "David Reubeni: An Early Visitor to Sennar," *Sudan Notes and Records*, 16: 55–56.

17. Jay Spaulding, *The Heroic Age in Sennar* (Trenton, N.J.: The Red Sea Press, 2007).

18. Rex S. O'Fahey, *State and Society in Dar Fur*, 4–5.

19. Robin Neillands, *The Dervish Wars, Gordon and Kitchener in the Sudan, 1880–1898* (London: John Murray, 1996), 66.

20. Douglas H. Johnson, "Recruitment and Entrapment in Private Slave Armies: The Structure of the Zariba in the Southern Sudan," *Slavery and Abolition*, 13: 1 (April 1992), 162–173.

21. Fergus Nicoll, *The Sword of the Prophet, The Mahdi of the Sudan and the Death of General Gordon* (UK: Sutton publishing, 2004), 7.

22. Neillands, *The Dervish Wars*, 155.

23. See John Iliffe, *A Modern History of Tanganyika* (Cambridge, U.K. and New York: Cambridge University Press, 1979).

24. "Our Power," Victoria to Sir Henry Ponsonby, Feb. 5, 1885, George E. Buckle, ed., *The Letters of Queen Victoria* (London: John Murray, 1928), 3: 598; this and Gladstone cited in Dominic Green,

Three Empires on the Nile: The Victorian Jihad, 1869–1899 (New York: Free Press, 2007), 199.

25. The Khalifa's final council took place shortly before midnight. His generals were desperate to avoid another daylight encounter with the British and pressed him to endorse another night attack. The most articulate advocate of this strategy was Ibrahim al-Khalil, a young amir from the nomadic Rizeigat clan of the western territories. The most celebrated Ansar general, Osman Digna, the hero of the Red Sea uprising years before, provided him with support. "By Allah, these English," he said. He had known them for fifteen years and thought they should be attacked by night. "You cannot beat the English without deceit." Osman Digna argued that the Ansar had always won in battle with a combination of surprise and shock, creeping forward, using darkness and natural cover where possible, before launching the final charge from close quarters, usually as dawn was breaking. To attack in open terrain in broad daylight would be brave but suicidal. The counterargument was led by the Khalifa's son, 'Osman' Sheikh al-Din, commander of his father's personal bodyguard, the Mulazimin, under the Green Banner. The dispute became heated, before the Khalifa—supported, as always, by his brother, Yaqub, commander of the Black Flag division—issued the final order: "We fight in the morning after prayers" (Green, 258). See also: L. Carl Brown, "The Sudanese Mah-diya," in Robert L. Rotberg and Ali A. Mazrui, eds., *Protest and Power in Black Africa* (New York: Oxford University Press, 1970), 147. For an early example of the Mahdi urging followers to follow these examples: Muhammad I. Abu Salim, *Al-Athar Al-Kamila lil Imam al-Mahdi*, vol. 1 (Khartoum: Khartoum University Press, 1993), 162–164. See also Dr. Fisal Muhammad Musa, "Judiciary and the Nile Fleet in the Mahadiya State in Sudan" (lecture given at Fifth International Conference on Sudan Studies at Durham University, 1999; Aharon Layish, "The Legal Methodology of the Mahdi," *Sudanic Africa* (1997), 8: 37–66.

26. British sources estimated that of the Khalifa's 52,000-strong fighting force, an estimated 12,800 were killed and as many as 16,000 wounded. Casualties in the British brigade amounted to twenty-eight killed and 147 wounded. In addition, there were said to be twenty

killed and 281 wounded among the British officers and "native troops" of the Egyptian and Sudanese regiments. Heather Sharkey, "A Jihad of the Pen: Mahdiya History and Historiography" (unpublished, draft lecture, November 18, 1993), 5, cited in Fergus Nicoll, *The Sword of the Prophet, The Mahdi of the Sudan and the Death of General Gordon*, 5.

27. Neillands, *The Dervish Wars*, 211.

28. Ibid., 213.

29. See Thomas Keneally, *Bettany's Book* (London: Sceptre, 2001), 85, 6; Fergus Nicoll, *The Sword of the Prophet, The Mahdi of the Sudan and the Death of General Gordon* (UK: Sutton publishing, 2004), 3–6.

30. Neillands, *The Dervish Wars*, 213–214, 215–216.

31. Maine, *Lectures on the Early History*, 330.

32. Peter A. Brunt, *Roman Imperial Themes* (New York: Oxford University Press, 1990), 114–115.

33. Ibid., 317.

34. It is worth noting the arguments advanced in favor of extending Roman citizenship in the debate that took place in the senate during Claudius's reign on whether to allow Comatan Gauls to stand for senatorial office. One of the three grounds that Claudius advanced for the admission of the Gauls was "that it was ancient Roman tradition to admit foreigners into the Roman state." Greg Woolf, *Becoming Roman: The Origins of Provincial Civilization in Gaul* (New York: Cambridge University Press, 2000), 64.

35. Andrew Lintot, *Imperium Romanum* (New York: Routledge, 1997), 161.

36. Martin Goodman, *Rome and Jerusalem, The Clash of Ancient Civilizations* (New York: Random House, Vintage Books, 2008), 156–158.

37. Brunt, *Roman Imperial Themes*, 118.

38. Martin Goodman, *Rome and Jerusalem, The Clash of Ancient Civilizations* (New York: Random House, Vintage Books, 2008), 157.

39. Lintot, *Imperium Romanum*, 167.

40. In addition, privileged communities were granted the status of "free" cities by senatorial decree Lintot, *Imperium Romanum*, 154.

41. "Originally these included the right to migrate to Rome and take up Roman citizenship at the expense of losing that of their

original community, but this privilege was suppressed early in the 2nd century BC at the request of the Latins themselves, concerned at their depopulation." Lintot, *Imperium Romanum*, 161.

42. Adrian N. Sherwin-White, *The Roman Citizenship* (New York: Oxford University Press, 1973), 150.

43. Leonard A. Curchin, *The Romanization of Central Spain: Complexity, Diversity and Change in a Provincial Hinterland* (London and New York: Routledge, 2004), 123.

44. Lintot, *Imperium Romanum*, 130–131.

45. Sherwin-White, *The Roman Citizenship*, 411.

46. Brunt, *Roman Imperial Themes*, 267–268.

47. Martin Goodman, *Rome and Jerusalem, The Clash of Ancient Civilizations* (New York: Random House, Vintage Books, 2008), 53–54.

48. Ibid., 438–439.

49. Benjamin Isaac, *The Limits of Empire: The Roman Army in the East* (New York: Oxford University Press, 1990), 83.

50. "Perhaps in the end the most important lesson we should learn from the Roman empire is not to claim too much for it. Roman power did bring coherence, but not the coherence of a city, a nation-state, or even a league of states with a regular constitution. The fact that we tend to idealize it as a universal society owes something to contemporary statements, such as those found in Aelius Aristeides, but far more to a tradition that grew up in the late empire, of which we are the heirs—one which sprang first from the Christian view of Rome a world-empire, whose destiny it was to prepare the way for the kingdom of God. According to this perception, when, under Constantine, the Christian world and the Roman world became coterminous, *ipso facto* Christendom became a universal society." Lintot, *Imperium Romanum*, 193.

51. Greg Woolf, *Becoming Roman: The Origins of Provincial Civilization in Gaul* (New York: Cambridge University Press, 2000), 68.

52. Woolf, *Becoming Roman*, 54–58. As Woolf rightly notes: "the development of the notion of humanitas can be seen as part of the Roman response to the cultural anxieties generated by the encounter with Greek culture over the last two centuries BC."

53. Woolf, *Becoming Roman*, 58–60.

54. Ibid., 18.

55. Jane Webster (1996), 11; Patrick Le Roux (1995), 17; Simon Keay (2001), 120; Greg Woolf (2001), 174; all cited in Leonard A. Curchin, *The Romanization of Central Spain: Complexity, Diversity and Change in a Provincial Hinterland*, (London and New York: Routledge, 2004), 8–14, 23.

56. In sharp contrast with claims by Henry Maine is the picture of Britain "described by the majority of English writers" as "a province in which Roman and native were as distinct as modern Englishman and Indian" in the modern British empire. In the words of a contemporary writer, "the departure of the Romans" in the fifth-century found Britons "almost as Celtic" as they had been at the time of Roman arrival. Francis Haverfield, *The Romanization of Roman Britain*, 2nd ed. (Oxford at the Clarendon Press, 1912), 19.

57. Brunt, *Roman Imperial Themes*, 111.

58. Benjamin Isaac, *The Limits of Empire: The Roman Army in the East* (New York: Oxford University Press, 1990), 1–2. It is only in the postcolonial period that former colonial powers faced the question of, as Isaac phrases it, "absorbing into their own society great numbers of their former subjects," and with great difficulty, too.

59. Ibid., 2.

60. Lintot, *Imperium Romanum*, 18.

61. Woolf, *Becoming Roman*, 18.

62. Brunt, *Roman Imperial Themes*, 122.

63. Ibid., 133.

THREE *Beyond Settlers and Natives*

1. Ikaweba Bunting, "The Heart of Africa: Interview with Nyerere on Anti-Colonialism," in Haroub Othman, ed., *Sites of Memory, Julius Nyerere and the Liberation Struggle of South Africa* (Zanzibar International Film Festival, 2007), 68.

2. Sabo Bako, "Education and Adjustment in Nigeria: Conditionalisty and Resistance," in Mamadou Diouf and Mahmood Mamdani, eds., *Academic Freedom in Africa* (Dakar, Senegal: CODESRIA, 1994), 150–175.

3. If Yusuf Bala Usman had been at a university with a wider reach, serviced by a galaxy of journals and libraries, and the focus of intense media attention, he would surely have attained a global stature. The sad fact is that Usman's writings were hardly known outside his own country, certainly not at the East and South African universities where I spent the early and middle part of my teaching career. Here, I will focus on Usman's key historical writings.

4. Yusuf Bala Usman, "The Assessment of Primary Sources: Heinrich Barth in Katsina, 1851–1854," in *Beyond Fairy Tales: Selected Historical Writings of Yusufu Bala Usman* (Zaria: Abdullahi Smith Centre for Historical Research, 2006), 1: 2–3.

5. Usman, "The Assessment of Primary Sources: Heinrich Barth in Katsina, 1851–1854," 13–14.

6. Usman, "History, Tradition and Reaction: The Perception of Nigerian History in the 19th and 20th Centuries," in *Beyond Fairy Tales*, 1: 41, 42.

7. Usman, "History, Tradition and Reaction: The Perception of Nigerian History in the 19th and 20th Centuries," in *Beyond Fairy Tales*, 1: 41, 42. [[Suggest changing this footnote to Ibid. A new footnote preceding this has been inserted into the text.]]

8. Usman, "The Assessment of Primary Sources," 21–22.

9. Ibid., 21.

10. Usman, "History, Tradition and Reaction," 21–22, 43.

11. Ibid., 63.

12. Usman, "The Assessment of Primary Sources," 6–7.

13. Ibid., 14–15.

14. Usman, "History, Tradition and Reaction," 42–43.

15. Ibid., 44–49.

16. Ibid., 56–57.

17. Ibid., 44.

18. Ibid., 61.

19. Usman, "The Problem of Ethnic Categories in the Study of the Historical Development of the Central Sudan: A Critique of M. G. Smith and Others," in *Beyond Fairy Tales*, 1: 23–24.

20. Ibid., 31.

21. Ibid., 28.

22. Usman, "Nations, Nation-States and the Future of Mankind: Some Observations on the Historical Experience of the Formation of the Kanawa in the 2nd Millennium A.D.," in *Beyond Fairy Tales*, 1: 153.

23. Usman, "The Problem of Ethnic Categories," 29.

24. Ibid., 37.

25. Ibid., 31.

26. Ibid., 37.

27. Ibid., 38.

28. See Kenneth O. Dike, *Trade and Politics in the Niger Delta, 1830–1885: An Introduction to the Economic and Political History of Nigeria* (Oxford: Clarendon Press), 30–31.

29. Ibid., 130.

30. Ibid., 7; see Usman, 133.

31. Usman, "Some Notes on the Three Basic Weaknesses in the Study of African Cultural History," in *Beyond Fairy Tales*, 66–67.

32. Roland Oliver and John D. Fage, *A Short History of Africa* (New York, 1963) 44, 45, 46, 51; quoted in Usman, "Abdullahi Smith and State Formation in the Central Sudan: The Limitations of Kinship and the Evasions of Fage and Oliver," in *Beyond Fairy Tales*, 1: 81.

33. Usman, "Abdullahi Smith and State Formation in the Central Sudan," 86.

34. Abdullahi Smith, "Some Considerations Relating to the Formation of States in Hausaland" in *A Little New Light: Selected Historical Writings of Abdullahi Smith* (Zaria: The Abdullahi Smith Centre for Historical Research, 1987), 1: 59–79; see Usman, "Abdullahi Smith and State Formation in the Central Sudan," 84.

35. Usman, "History, Tradition and Reaction," 58.

36. His thesis was published as Yusuf Bala Usman, *The Transformation of Katsina, 1400–1883, The Emergence and Overthrow of the Sarauta System and the Establishment of the Emirate* (ABU Press, 1981).

37. *Appreciation* (Unpublished booklet by students of Yusuf Bala Usman), 21, citing Usman, "History and Challenges to the Peoples and Polities of Africa in the 21st Century" (Dike Memorial Lecture, Nov. 22, 1999).

38. *Appreciation*, 24, citing Usman, *The Misrepresentation of Nigeria*, 2000.

39. See my *Citizen and Subject: Contemporary Africa and the Legacy of Late Colonialism* (Princeton: Princeton University Press, 1996).

40. Usman's intervention in the debate was described as follows by his students: "This lecture was a devastating blow at those clamouring for a so-called sovereign national conference, where self-appointed tribal champions would restructure Nigeria into a federation of nationalities and ethnic groups. He showed that the advocates of such a conference, such as professor Wole Soyinka, were not only deeply ignorant of the historical processes which had produced, and continued to shape, both the Nigerian polity as well as the ethnic groups which constituted it, they were also unaware of the simple fact that these ethnic groups had, in reality, no boundaries that could be demarcated because they intermeshed into one another at the levels of culture, language, territory and identity." See *Appreciation*, 22, Usman, "History and Challenges to the Peoples and Polities of Africa in the 21st Century" (Dike Memorial Lecture, Nov. 22, 1999).

41. "Passing on the Tongs," excerpts from a speech by Mwalimu Julius K. Nyerere to Parliament in Dar es Salaam on July 29, 1985, in Tanzania Standard (Newspapers) Ltd., *Nyerere: 1961–1985 . . . Passing on the Tongs*, Dar es Salaam: Tanzania Standard (Newspapers) Ltd. (1986), 52.

42. Such as Amir Jamal, Sophia Mustafa, and Mahmood Rattansey.

43. H. G. Mwakyembe, "The Parliament and the Electoral Process," in Issa G. Shivji, ed., *The State and the Working People in Tanzania* (CODESRIA, 1986), 21–22; (Pratt, 1960); Arnold J. Temu, "The Rise and Triumph of Nationalism," in *A History of Tanzania*, ed. Isaria N. Kimambo and Arnold J. Temu (Nairobi: East African Publishing House, 1969), 211.

44. James Clagett Taylor, *The Political Development of Tanganyika* (Stanford University Press, 1963), 138, 159.

45. National Archives: Accession 540, 17C, cited in Ronald Aminzade, "The Politics of Race and Nation: Citizenship and

Africanization in Tanganyika" (2001); *Political Power and Social Theory*, vol. 14 (Greenwich, CT: JAI Press).

46. Hugh W. Stephens, *The Political Transformation of Tanganyika: 1920–1967* (New York: Praeger, 1968), 110.

47. Judith Listowel, *The Making of Tanganyika* (Chatto and Windus, 1965), 378.

48. Tanganyika National Assembly Debates (1961), 333–334, 364, cited in "the Politics of Race and Nation: Citizenship and Africanization in Tanganyika," *Political Power and Social Theory*.

49. African National Congress Press Release of 1962, National Archives, Accession 561, 17, cited in "The Politics of Race and Nation: Citizenship and Africanization in Tanganyika," *Political Power and Social Theory* (Taylor, 1963), 194; Irving Kaplan. *Tanzania: A Country Study* (Washington, D.C.: American University, 1978), 72; Pratt, Cranford, *The Critical Phase in Tanzania 1945–1968* (Cambridge: Cambridge University Press, 1976), 92, 106.

50. Judith Listowel, *The Making of Tanganyika* (Chatto and Windus, 1965), 412.

51. Andrew Coulson, *Tanzania: A Political Economy* (Clarendon Press, 1982), 139.

52. Mwesiga Baregu, "Political Culture and the Party State in Tanzania," *Southern Review*, vol. 9 no. 1 (October 1995), 32.

53. *Tanganyika Standard* (May 9 and January 4, 1963).

54. *Tanganyika Standard* (January 8, 1964); Listowel, *The Making of Tanganyika*, 416–417.

55. National Archives, Accession 561, 17; cited in Ronald Aminzade, "The Politics of Race and Nation: Citizenship and Africanization in Tanganyika" (2001). *Political Power and Social Theory*, vol. 14 (Greenwich, CT: JAI Press).

56. Annie Smyth and Adam Seftel, eds., *Tanzania: The Story of Julius Nyerere, Through the Pages of DRUM* (Kampala: Fountain Publishers Ltd., 1993), 100–102, 104–105.

57. Julius K. Nyerere, *Freedom and Unity* (Dar es Salaam: Oxford, 1967), 70.

58. Nyerere, *Crusade for Liberation* (Dar es Salaam: Oxford University Press, 1978), 10.

59. See Issa Shivji, *Class Struggles in Tanzania* (Dar es Salaam: Tanzania Publishing House, 1976).

60. Mwalimu Julius K. Nyerere, *The Arusha Declaration Teach-In* (Dar es Salaam: The Information Services, 1967), 1.

61. Ikaweba Bunting, "The Heart of Africa: Interview with Nyerere on Anti-Colonialism," in Haroub Othman, ed., *Sites of Memory, Julius Nyerere and the Liberation Struggle of South Africa* (Zanzibar International Film Festival, 2007), 67.

62. Smythe and Seftel, eds., *Tanzania: The Story of Julius Nyerere*, 146-147.

63. Ibid., 146-148.

64. Ibid., 148-149.

65. "The decentralization reform in Tanzania 1972 is probably the most extensive effort to reshape an unintegrated prefectoral system along the lines of the prefectoral model." Goran Hyden, *No Shortcuts to Progress: African Development Management in Perspective* (Nairobi: Heinemann Educational Books, 1983), 90.

66. "Because of Tanzania's good relationship with a wide range of countries, it was possible for each region to be 'adopted' by one donor agency who took on itself to prepare a regional development plan—in some cases with no local involvement at all—and to provide development funds." Goran Hyden, *No Shortcuts to Progress: African Development Management in Perspective*, 91.

67. "Passing on the Tongs," excerpts from a speech by Mwalimu Julius K. Nyerere, to Parliament in Dar es Salaam on July 29, 1985, in Tanzania Standard (Newspapers) Ltd., *Nyerere: 1961-1985*, 54.

68. "The magistracy has been separated from the administration, all magistrates must now have some rudimentary training before starting on their duties, an increased number of magistrates have been appointed, and so far as possible sufficient court houses established to secure easy access for everyone." John P. W. B. McAuslan and Yash P. Ghai, "Constitutional Innovation and Political Stability in Tanzania:

A Preliminary Assessment," in Lionel Cliffe and John S. Saul, *Socialism in Tanzania*, vol. 1: Politics (Dar es Salaam: East African Publishing House, 1972), 199.

69. "Passing on the Tongs, excerpts from a speech by Mwalimu Julius K. Nyerere, to Parliament in Dar es Salaam on July 29, 1985, in Tanzania Standard (Newspapers) Ltd., *Nyerere: 1961-1985*, 52.

70. Arkadi Glukhov, "The Fateful August of 1968, Hot Summer in Dar es Salaam, A Political Profile of Julius Kambarage Nyerere," Russian Academy of Sciences, Institute for African Studies, *Julius Nyerere: Humanist, Politician, Thinker*, trans. B. G. Petruk, (Dar es Salaam: Mkuki na Nyota, 2005), 46-47.

71. Nyerere, *Crusade for Liberation* (Dar es Salaam: Oxford University Press, 1978), 11, 13.

Acknowledgments

The provocation to think in comparative terms came from Professor Andreas Ashete, former Vice Chancellor of Addis Ababa University. For helpful guidance on the literature on the Roman empire, I thank Marco Maiuro of the Department of History at Columbia University. For introducing me to the literature around *adat*, I thank Lilianne Fann, my graduate student at the department of anthropology at Columbia. For editorial and library assistance, I thank Doris Carrion, graduate student in the department of history at Columbia University. For helping with routine responsibilities so I could find the time to clean up these lectures, I thank Doreen Tazwaire at Makerere Institute of Social Research in Kampala and Tarik Chelali at the School of Public and International Affairs at Columbia University.

I dedicate the lectures with love to Mira, affectionately known to Zohran and me as *Wawa*, from the Gujarati *wawajodu*, a compelling force of nature.

149

Index

* 9 7 8 0 6 7 4 0 5 0 5 2 5 *